MEDIAEVAL SOURCES
IN TRANSLATION

27

St. Thomas Aquinas

QUODLIBETAL QUESTIONS 1 AND 2

Translated with an Introduction and Notes

by

SANDRA EDWARDS

PONTIFICAL INSTITUTE OF MEDIAEVAL STUDIES

The publishing program of the
Pontifical Institute is supported
through the generosity of
the De Rancé Foundation.

CANADIAN CATALOGUING IN PUBLICATION DATA

Thomas, Aquinas, Saint, 1225?-1274.
  [Quaestiones de quodlibet.   1-2.   English]
  Quodlibetal questions 1 and 2

(Mediaeval sources in translation, ISSN 0316-0874 ; 27)
Bibliography: p.
Includes index.
ISBN 0-88844-276-9

1. Theology - Middle Ages, 600-1500 - Miscellanea.   I. Edwards,
Sandra, 1944-   II. Pontifical Institute of Mediaeval Studies.
III. Title.   IV. Title: Quaestiones de quodlibet.   1-2.   English.
V. Series.

B765.T52E5 1983   189´.4   C83-094011-1

Pontifical Institute of Mediaeval Studies
59 Queen's Park Crescent East
Toronto, Ontario, Canada M5S 2C4

PRINTED BY UNIVERSA PRESS, WETTEREN, BELGIUM

Contents

Abbreviations

Ad Cor. (Hebr., Rom., Tit.)	St. Thomas Aquinas, *Expositio et lectura super epistolas Pauli apostoli* (Taurino, 1953)
BGPMA	*Beiträge zur Geschichte der Philosophie und Theologie des Mittelalters* (Münster, 1891 –)
CC	Corpus Christianorum series latina, Continuatio mediaevalis (Turnholti, 1953 –)
CG	St. Thomas Aquinas, *Summa contra gentiles*, Leonine ed., vols. 13-15 (Rome, 1918-1930)
Comp. theol.	St. Thomas Aquinas, *Compendium theologiae*, Leonine ed., vol. 42 (Rome, 1976)
Contra errores Graecorum	St. Thomas Aquinas, *Contra errores Graecorum*, Leonine ed., vol. 40 (Rome, 1967)
CSEL	*Corpus scriptorum ecclesiasticorum latinorum*, ed. G. Schepps and S. Brandt (Vienna, 1866-1913)
De duabus naturis	Boethius, *Liber contra Eutychen et Nestorium*, ed. E. K. Rand, *The Theological Tractates* (Cambridge, Mass., 1918), pp. 72-128; PL 64: 1337-1354
De div. nom.	St. Thomas Aquinas, *Expositio super Dionysium de divinis nominibus*, ed. C. Pera and P. Caramello (Taurino, 1950)
De hebdomadibus	Boethius, *Quomodo substantiae in eo quod sint bonae sint*, ed. E. K. Rand, *The Theological Tractates* (Cambridge, Mass., 1918), pp. 38-50; PL 64: 1311-1314
De perfect. vitae spirit.	St. Thomas Aquinas, *De perfectione spiritualis vitae*, Leonine ed., vol. 41 (Rome, 1970)
De potentia	St. Thomas Aquinas, *Quaestiones disputatae de potentia*, ed. P. M. Pession (Taurino, 1953)
De sep. subs.	Thomas Aquinas, *De substantiis separatis*, ed. F. J. Lescoe (West Hartford, Conn., 1962)

De ver.	St. Thomas Aquinas, *Quaestiones disputatae de veritate*, Leonine ed., vol. 22 (Rome, 1970-1974)
In Boeth. de hebdom.	St. Thomas Aquinas, *Expositio in librum Boethii de hebdomadibus*, Marietti ed. (Taurino, 1954)
In De hebdomadibus	See *In Boeth. de hebdom.* above
In Ioann.	St. Thomas Aquinas, *Super evangelium Johannis lectura*, ed. P. R. Cai (Taurino, 1952)
In Mathaeum, In Matth.	St. Thomas Aquinas, *Super evangelium Matthaei expositio*, ed. P. Cai (Taurino, 1951)
In Ps.	St. Thomas Aquinas, *Postilla super Psalmos*, Parma ed., vol. 18 (Parma, c. 1865)
In meta.	St. Thomas Aquinas, *In XII libros metaphysicorum expositio*, ed. M.-R. Cathala (Taurino, 1935)
PG	Patrologia Graeco-Latina, ed. Jacques-Paul Migne, Patrologiae Cursus Completus (Paris, 1844-1864; repr. Turnholti, 1958-1972)
PL	Patrologia Latina, in Patrologiae Cursus Completus as above
Quaest. de anima	St. Thomas Aquinas, *Quaestiones de anima*, ed. J. H. Robb (Toronto, 1968)
Sent.	Peter Lombard, *Libri IV sententiarum* (2nd ed., Quaracchi, 1916) but also the commentaries on the *Sentences* of St. Bonaventure, St. Thomas Aquinas, etc. (see Bibliography)
Spir. Creat.	St. Thomas Aquinas, *De spiritualibus creaturis*, ed. L. Keeler (Rome, 1946)
ST	St. Thomas Aquinas, *Summa theologiae*, Blackfriars ed. (Latin and English transl.) (New York, 1964-1969)
Suppl.	St. Thomas Aquinas, *Supplementum* to *Summa theologiae*, Leonine ed., vol. 12 (Rome, 1906)

Introduction

I

St. Thomas began his career at the University of Paris as a bachelor in theology in 1252. Although normally such a bachelor began his teaching duties as a *baccalaureus biblicus*, reading and commenting cursorily on the Bible to classes of undergraduates for two years, this requirement seems to have been waived in St. Thomas's case (possibly because he had already done such commentaries previously in Dominican houses), and he was admitted at the age of twenty-seven as a senior bachelor or *baccalaureus sententiarius*. In such capacity he would lecture and comment upon the four books of Peter Lombard's *Sententiae*, a basic text in theology, for several years. During the time prior to receiving his master's degree, a bachelor had also to participate in both ordinary and extraordinary disputes. Presumably St. Thomas fulfilled this and all other requirements for he incepted (i.e., underwent formal graduation exercises) in 1256 and became a master of theology, moving into one of the two teaching positions established for members of the Dominican order on the theology faculty at Paris.[1]

St. Thomas assumed his teaching duties as regent master in the fall of 1256. These duties included delivering sermons, lecturing on texts, and holding disputes.[2] The lecture or *lectio* was the traditional method of teaching and for a master of theology it consisted of reading passages of the Bible aloud to a class, analyzing and commenting

---

[1] For a fuller description of the bachelor stages in theology, see Palémon Glorieux, "L'enseignement au Moyen Âge. Techniques et méthodes en usage à la Faculté de théologie de Paris au xiiie siècle," *Archives d'histoire doctrinale et littéraire du Moyen Âge* 43 (1968), 65-186. On St. Thomas's career in particular, see James A. Weisheipl, *Friar Thomas d'Aquino: His Life, Thought, and Work* (New York, 1974), chapter 2, and Angelus Walz, *Saint Thomas Aquinas: A Biographical Study*, transl. S. Bullough (Westminster, Md., 1951), chapter 6.

[2] Weisheipl, *Friar Thomas*, p. 116.

upon them, and selecting certain questions arising out of the text for further exploration and discussion with the class.[3] Only masters could engage in these extensive commentaries; a *biblicus* had the right only to read and comment cursorily.[4] A master was also required to hold ordinary disputes or *quaestiones disputatae* from time to time. He would submit a list of questions on some topic of his choice to be discussed with his students and other masters, and would set a time for the dispute.[5] On that day all lectures by other masters would be cancelled. All bachelors had to attend and some of them, either those under the supervision of the presiding master or those of other masters, were assigned roles as respondents or opponents. They in fact did most of the work in the first stage of what Mandonnet calls "a tournament of clerics." [6] *Biblici* and *sententiarii*, i.e., both junior and senior bachelors, were required to participate in such disputes of their own or other masters a specified number of times before being permitted to incept. A thesis was proposed by the *responsalis* or responding bachelor, objections to the thesis were raised, and the *responsalis* replied to these. The presiding master could participate as he saw fit, directing the discussion, making suggestions, correcting, etc. After the objection-response session, a second or magistral session was held in which the master himself went over all that had transpired during the previous discussion, coordinating the objections and responses to them, and giving his *determinatio* or definitive answer to the question followed by his responses to the objections which had been raised against his thesis. Only masters had the right to give determinations.

An ordinary dispute did not consist of just the two sessions sketched above. There would be a whole series of questions to be discussed and determined:

> Every master held them several times a year, and these were closely connected with his lectures. The characteristic feature of the *dispu-*

---

[3] Chenu, *Toward Understanding St. Thomas*, transl. A. M. Landry and W. D. Hughes (New York, 1964), pp. 79-88; Weisheipl, *Friar Thomas*, pp. 116-123.

[4] Glorieux, "L'enseignement," p. 119.

[5] The details on the procedure for disputed questions are found in Glorieux, ibid., pp. 123-128; Weisheipl, *Friar Thomas*, pp. 123-126; Chenu, *Toward Understanding*, pp. 88-91; and Lottie H. Kendzierski, in her "Introduction" to St. Thomas Aquinas's *On Charity* (Milwaukee, 1960), pp. 3-6.

[6] Mandonnet, preface to the *Quaestiones quodlibetales* (Paris, 1925), p. ii.

tationes ordinariae is the weighty, difficult, and related themes, often representing a large and uniform complexity of questions, which were discussed with all the thoroughness of scholastic research. On such a comprehensive subject, many *disputationes ordinariae* could be arranged, sometimes extending over a period of several years.[7]

Disputed questions sometimes exist today only in *reportationes* or versions derived from student notes; many, however, exist also in *ordinationes* or versions written by the master himself, perhaps years after the dispute.[8] St. Thomas held many ordinary disputes on such diverse topics as truth, evil, the power of God, the virtues, spiritual creatures, and the soul, both in Paris and in Italy, and by their means explored in depth some of the questions later taken up and given more summary treatment in his *Summa theologiae*.[9]

In addition to the required lectures, ordinary disputes, and sermons, a master could if he wished periodically hold extraordinary disputes as well. These were already established parts of academic life by the time St. Thomas began his studies at Paris, and he would have found himself almost immediately involved in them as a *sententiarius*.[10] Unlike the ordinary disputes which focussed on a single topic, the extraordinary disputes could involve questions on any topic however remotely related to theology. These thus came to be called *quaestiones quodlibetales* or questions on any subject (*de quolibet*). The questions arose from the audience itself and were not predetermined by the presiding master although he might perhaps suggest questions for his own students to ask, and he could set a limit to the number of questions and refuse to answer some.[11] A master

---

[7] Kendzierski, Saint Thomas, *On Charity*, p. 3.

[8] Weisheipl, *Friar Thomas*, p. 117.

[9] Chenu, *Toward Understanding*, p. 285; Walz, *Saint Thomas*, pp. 74-75.

[10] At one time Mandonnet believed that St. Thomas had created the quodlibetal disputes (see his preface to the *Quaestiones quodlibetales* and his article "Thomas d'Aquin, créateur de la dispute quodlibétique," *Revue des sciences philosophiques et théologiques* 16 (1927), 5-38 and 15 (1926), 477-506). This view was later shown to be false by Glorieux, "Aux origines du Quodlibet," *Divus Thomas* 38 (1935), 502-522, and others. Quodlibetal disputes were held earlier in the century by such figures as Alexander of Hales and Robert Grosseteste.

[11] Details on the procedure for quodlibetal disputes are given by R. Spiazzi in his "Introductio" to the Marietti edition of the *Quaestiones quodlibetales* (Taurino, 1956), p. viii; by Mandonnet in his preface to his edition of the same work, pp. iv-v; Weisheipl, *Friar Thomas*, pp. 126-127; Glorieux, "L'enseignement," pp. 128-134;

had only to announce that he would hold a quodlibetal dispute during Advent or Lent, and an audience of bachelors fulfilling their degree requirements, other students, other masters, and perhaps some local church officials would be certain to gather at the appointed time. The procedure was similar to that for the ordinary disputes. Certain bachelors were designated as respondents and they took questions from the floor, proposed theses, and responded to objections raised from the floor. There was an element of surprise in the questions themselves which came in no fixed order and concerned no prearranged topic. The bachelors involved thus underwent an "ordeal by fire," getting the opportunity to show the depth and breadth of the learning they had so far acquired. Again the presiding master could intervene at will. On the next teaching day following the discussion session, there was a second or magistral session in which the master, having now classified the random questions into some kind of logical order and having coordinated the pro's and con's of the thesis on each question, offered his determination on each. Perhaps he also responded to the objections that had been raised against each thesis.[12] As with ordinary disputes, written versions exist in both *reportatio* and *ordinatio* forms.[13]

Many masters held quodlibetal disputes frequently, some did so occasionally, and a few apparently refused to hold any at all. The nature of the dispute was such as to make any in-depth discussion impossible. As a result, the determinations, unless considerably embellished later in the *ordinatio*, are briefer, the objections and responses fewer. There is an air of excitement, however, and many of the questions raised were timely ones which reflected current controversies both within and without the schools. Quodlibetal questions might range over topics as diverse as pastoral care, religious life, practical morality, theology, and the abstractions of philosophy. As Walz says, "The Quodlibeta demonstrate most forcibly the unity of the whole of medieval theology (exegesis, dogma, moral, liturgy, canon law, and the discussion of particular casus), and reflect a very

---

Chenu, *Toward Understanding*, pp. 91-93 and 285-287; Walz, *Saint Thomas*, p. 75; Leonard E. Boyle, "The Quodlibets of St. Thomas and Pastoral Care," *The Thomist* 38 (1974), 232-235.

[12] See Boyle, p. 236.

[13] Ibid., p. 235.

fine period in the history of thought and culture at the time. The Quodlibeta deal with problems of the moment, apologetics, and even personal matters." [14] As will be seen below, all of this applies not only to quodlibetal disputes in general but to those of St. Thomas in particular.

II

After becoming a master in 1256, St. Thomas began immediately holding quodlibetal disputes twice a year during his first Parisian regency (1256-1259). He continued to do so during his second Parisian regency (1269-1272). There are twelve quodlibeta in all, each a series of questions asked during one Advent or Lenten session. The customary numerical arrangement of these does not, however, reflect their original chronological order. Quodlibets 7-11 have been decisively shown by Mandonnet to belong to the first Parisian regency, while Quodlibets 1-6 (and possibly 12) have been shown to belong to the second regency.[15] There is considerable debate as to whether the numerical ordering within each of those two sets constitutes a chronological arrangement. This is especially true for Quodlibets 7-11.[16] As regards the second set, Pelster has argued that Quodlibet 3 preceded Quodlibet 2, and Weisheipl, van Steenberghen, and Mandonnet maintain that Quodlibet 12 came between Quodlibets 3 and 4.[17] Quodlibet 1 has been variously placed at either Lent 1269 or Advent 1269. Precise dating for each of the Quodlibets seems impossible, for it must usually be based on the relation of the questions to other works of St. Thomas, particularly the disputed

---

[14] Walz, *Saint Thomas*, p. 75.

[15] Mandonnet, preface pp. v-vi; and "Thomas d'Aquin, créateur"; Weisheipl, *Friar Thomas*, p. 127 and p. 367.

[16] See Boyle's summary chart of the different attempts to date the various Quodlibets, "The Quodlibets," p. 239. H. Denifle located the exact dates for both Quodlibet 3 and Quodlibet 5; see "Die Statuten der Juristen-Universität Bologna, I," *Archiv für Literatur und Kirchengeschichte des Mittelalters* 3 (1907), 320.

[17] F. Pelster, "Literarhistorische Probleme der Quodlibeta des Hl. Thomas von Aquin, II," *Gregorianum* 28 (1947), 63-69; Weisheipl, *Friar Thomas*, p. 367; Mandonnet, "Thomas d'Aquin, créateur"; and F. van Steenberghen, *Siger de Brabant dans l'histoire de l'aristotélisme* (Louvain, 1942), p. 541.

questions, and there is considerable controversy over the dating of many of these also.[18] The chart below summarizes the views concerning the dating of the second set of Quodlibets:

Quodlibet 1	1269 Lent, according to Mandonnet and others, though Pelster puts it at Advent 1269
Quodlibet 2	1269 Advent, according to most scholars, though Pelster places it at Advent 1270, following Quodlibet 3
Quodlibet 3	1270 Lent
Quodlibet 4	1271 Lent
Quodlibet 5	1271 Advent
Quodlibet 6	1272 Lent
Quodlibet 12	Mandonnet, van Steenberghen, and Weisheipl put this at Advent 1270, after Quodlibet 3.[19]

It has been demonstrated that some of the material incorporated into the editions of the *Quaestiones quodlibetales* of St. Thomas are not Quodlibets at all but disputed questions. These include Quodlibet 7, q. 6 on the meanings of Scripture (which may have been part of St. Thomas's inception disputes), Quodlibet 7, q. 7 which is a lengthy disputed question on manual labor in relation to religious, and Quodlibet 4, q. 12 which is a disputed question concerning the entrance of children into religious life.[20]

St. Thomas's written versions of the *Quaestiones quodlibetales* (except for that of Quodlibet 12 which may be a student's, or St. Thomas's, notes) reflect in format, though not in organization, the structure of the oral sessions.[21] St. Thomas has grouped the questions according to topic, and the major divisions are into questions concerning God, questions concerning angels, and questions concerning man. Each question is broken down into articles. The article is the true *quaestio* of the discussion session, and generally begins with the word "*Utrum*," i.e., "Utrum Christus in triduo mortis fuerit idem homo numero" ("Whether Christ was numerically the same man during the three days of death"). Next come the words "*Sic proceditur*," or "We proceed as follows," followed by the arguments or authorities which support one answer to the question raised. After

---

[18] Weisheipl, *Friar Thomas*, p. 125.
[19] This chart is adapted from data in Boyle, "The Quodlibets," p. 239, and Weisheipl, *Friar Thomas*, p. 367.
[20] Weisheipl, *Friar Thomas*, pp. 104-107.
[21] Boyle, "The Quodlibets," p. 236; Weisheipl, *Friar Thomas*, p. 367.

these comes the *"Sed contra,"* an argument (or perhaps several) or authority supporting another position on the same question. Next St. Thomas gives his determination, marked by the words *"Respondeo: Dicendum quod..."*, i.e., "I answer: It must be said that...." Last, his responses to the arguments given at the first which oppose all or part of his thesis are given with such words as the following: "Therefore, to the first it must be said that...." [22] His determinations are usually brief and to the point. They sketch arguments rather than present them in full, but many of these can be found more fully developed in his other works. This seems to indicate that in writing his *ordinatio* he did not elaborate much on what actually transpired during the oral sessions. The objections given at the start are usually few in number, and the *sed contra* often contains only one argument or authority.

Each of the Quodlibets covers a broad range of questions, reflecting both the interests of the audience and the interests and skills of the master.[23] These might concern current controversies, or even events outside the schools. Glorieux has shown that when they began, quodlibetal questions tended to be of a practical nature but became increasingly speculative as the decades passed.[24] With St. Thomas, however, the earlier Quodlibets (those of the first set, 7-11) contain far fewer practical questions than do those of the years 1269-1272.[25] In his case, the practical questions pertain to such matters as the giving of alms, prayers for the dead, marriage vows, confessions, fraternal correction, usury, deception in business transactions, papal constitutions, lying, tithes, crusades. More speculative in nature are the theological questions concerning such matters as the attributes and existence of God, the two natures in Christ, the Eucharist, grace. Philosophical questions deal with topics like the composition of angels, the nature of the human soul, the process of cognition. (The distinction between theological and philosophical questions is often an artificial one – a good deal of philosophical reasoning is involved in answering many of the theological questions, and many of the questions which appear largely philosophical have theological implications). Quite a few questions relate to religious life, either in

---

[22] See also Chenu, *Toward Understanding*, pp. 93-96.
[23] Boyle, "The Quodlibets," pp. 240-241.
[24] Glorieux, "L'enseignement," pp. 132-133.
[25] Boyle, "The Quodlibets," pp. 246-247.

itself or in relation to the secular priesthood. And, as Boyle has shown, many questions relate to pastoral care.[26] Several questions concern crusaders and may reflect the audience's interest in King Louis ix's crusade of 1270. Occasionally questions are frivolous in nature, reflecting perhaps the mentality of young undergraduates present at the dispute, e.g., "Whether truth is stronger than wine, king, or a woman?" (Quodlibet 12, q. 14, a.1), and "Whether someone can naturally or miraculously be simultaneously a virgin and a father" (Quodlibet 6, q. 10). Even these are given serious attention by St. Thomas. There are also some questions on teaching and the methods used in universities, e.g., "Whether those who hear diverse masters of theology who have contrary opinions are excused from sin if they follow the false opinions of their masters?" (Quodlibet 3, q. 4, a.2), "Whether, if a teacher always preached or taught principally for the sake of vainglory, he has a halo if he repents at death?" (Quodlibet 5, q. 12, a.1).

Within the two Quodlibets here presented, we find the following subjects:

Quodlibet 1: God – the divine essence, the nature of Christ
angels – their motion
man – the soul, grace, man's love for God, confession, plurality of prebends, teaching versus the direction of souls, obedience of religious, sin, perjury and homicide, obedience to papal constitutions, monastic life, the nature of glorified bodies
Quodlibet 2: God – Christ's death and suffering
angels – their composition and relation to time
man – belief in miracles, baptism of Jewish children, tithes, filial obedience, morality in business, seeking of offices, punishment after death, sin against the Holy Spirit, crusaders.

As will be seen below, several of these are concerned with controversies then current at the University of Paris.

The sources used in St. Thomas's two Quodlibets presented here are not as various as those in his other works, nor are they as

---

[26] Ibid.

numerous. This is undoubtedly due to the nature of the quodlibetal dispute which would not have permitted an extensive use of authorities. The Bible is cited most frequently – 78 times (23 from the Old Testament, 55 from the New); Biblical glosses are referred to five times. Aristotle is relied on somewhat more than is St. Augustine, receiving 24 citations to the latter's 18. Gregory the Great is cited six times, St. Bernard of Clairvaux six, and Averroes three times, while Peter Lombard, Boethius, St. Basil, St. Jerome, St. John Chrysostom, and Gratian are quoted or referred to twice each. Avicenna, Cicero, St. Ambrose, St. Anselm, St. Hilary, and Isidore of Seville are referred to once each. These numbers are fairly representative of the twelve Quodlibets as a whole, although in general St. Augustine is cited more often than Aristotle.

If they are not his most significant works, the *Quodlibetal Questions* are valuable for showing us a side of St. Thomas that is not so evident elsewhere. Here we see a master who could field questions of a very diverse sort and in responding almost always tie his answers in with his broader philosophical and theological doctrines. Thus if the subject matter has little in the way of unity, there is definite unification provided by the mind of the master himself. Often the responses shed some new light on his thought developed elsewhere, for the phrasing of the question itself might provide a new twist. Occasionally there are topics presented which he has not dealt with elsewhere, as is the case with the questions on crusaders. And occasionally his responses seem to have satisfied St. Thomas enough to be incorporated verbatim into other works as happened with Quodlibet 2, q. 4, a.2 on the baptism of Jewish children which will reappear in *Summa theologiae* 2-2 in almost exactly the same language. As has been noted above, arguments are usually sketched rather than developed fully. It is interesting to speculate whether those he sketches here (and he does omit arguments used elsewhere, presenting for example only one of the major arguments for the unicity of substantial form in man in Quodlibet 1, q. 4, a.1) are those he thought the most convincing in general, or whether they are the ones he thought most suitable for the audience and occasion of the dispute.

Apparently the *Quodlibetal Questions*, as written works, were not particularly influential after St. Thomas left Paris in 1272. Leonard Boyle has shown, however, that the many questions on pastoral care in the second set received wide circulation via the *Summa confessorum* of John of Freiburg which drew heavily on them.[27]

III

Several of the articles contained in Quodlibets 1 and 2 are of particular interest because they reflect controversies in which St. Thomas was engaged in the first year of his second Parisian regency. Thus we find questions bearing on the second Antimendicant controversy, and on the issue of the unicity of substantial form. None of the articles is concerned with matters relating to Averroism, however, although this was a topic of heated debate and St. Thomas was to address it directly in 1270 in his treatise against the unicity of the intellect.

St. Thomas returned to Paris in 1269 because of a renewal of the Antimendicant controversy which had so influenced his earlier stay in Paris. The complaints of the secular clergy remained much the same as before: they were disturbed by the mendicant orders' encroachment on what they considered their prerogatives of preaching, hearing confessions, directing souls, and collecting fees and donations: they resented the fact that the friars were not subject to control by the local bishops.[28] After the Dominican and Franciscan Orders were established in Paris earlier in the century, their members acquired a reputation for good preaching. The secular masters resisted their entrance into university circles though the mendicants acquired two chairs in theology when secular masters joined the orders. Soon a reputation for fine teaching by the orders was established as well. Resentment developed into a slander campaign which created enough tension for King Louis ix to feel it necessary to send his troops in to protect the members of the two orders in 1252. Although the popes supported the position of the mendicants and their right to the chairs in theology, the university guild of masters refused admission to the mendicant masters, including St. Thomas. William of St. Amour in particular wrote many works against the two orders. The pope, however, remained generally supportive and

---

[27] Ibid., pp. 252 ff.

[28] See Vernon J. Bourke, *Aquinas' Search for Wisdom* (Milwaukee, 1965), chapter 7, and Weisheipl, *Friar Thomas*, pp. 80-92.

exiled William from Paris in 1257 while insisting that the mendicant masters be permitted to enter the guild.[29]

After the condemnation of William of St. Amour, the controversy died down only to reappear again in 1269 in the quodlibetal disputes held by his follower Gerard d'Abbeville. Gerard basically maintained that both archdeacons and parish priests are in the state of perfection, and are more perfect than members of religious orders.[30] St. Thomas responded to Gerard's claims in a separate treatise, *De perfectione spiritualis vitae*, and also in his own quodlibetal disputes. While he addressed the issue briefly in Quodlibet 1, q. 7, a.2, a more thorough treatment is to be found later in Quodlibet 3, q. 6, a.3, "Whether the state of religious life is more perfect than the state of parish priests and archdeacons?" St. Thomas responds first of all by saying that the measure of the spiritual perfection of a life is charity. From this it follows that perfection consists in holding oneself and one's possessions in contempt for the sake of God. This is true whether one is secular or religious, cleric or laymen – even a married person. Yet being perfect is not necessarily a matter of being in a state of perfection: "For some are in a state of perfection who are never perfect but sometimes even sinners; some also are perfect who are not in a state of perfection."[31] Now a state (*status*) is a condition of freedom or servitude. So those are properly said to be in a state of perfection who put themselves in servitude in order to fulfill the works of perfection. This placing oneself in subjection is accomplished through a vow. Religious take solemn vows of obedience, poverty, chastity while bishops in their consecration, obligate their whole lives to perfection and caring for their flocks. But archdeacons and priests have taken no such vows nor have they been consecrated like bishops. They have duties, of course, as a result of ordination, but are not obligated to perfection. They are free to give up their parishes so their commitments are not perpetual. It is otherwise with the state of perfection which no one can leave without sinning mortally. Arch-

---

[29] All information on this controversy comes from Bourke, *Aquinas' Search*, and Weisheipl, *Friar Thomas*. The latter describes the various stages of development in great detail.

[30] Bourke, *Aquinas' Search*, p. 177. For more detail on the second controversy, see Weisheipl, *Friar Thomas*, pp. 263-272.

[31] *Quaestiones quodlibetales*, ed. Spiazzi. The translation is mine.

deacons and priests may do particular laudable works which are greater than any religious perform, but all in all the state of the religious is higher because of the perpetual obligation to give all to God: "If someone totally and perfectly increases his own salvation, it is much greater than if someone does many particular works for the salvation of others." [32]

Similar reasoning may be found in *Summa theologiae* 2-2, 184 and in the treatise *De perfectione spiritualis vitae*. The dispute is tied in with the teaching profession in Quodlibet 1, q. 7, a.2, on "Whether somone is bound to give up the study of theology, even if he is suited to teaching others, in order to devote himself to the salvation of souls?" Using an analogy between the Church and a building, St. Thomas says that architects and planners of buildings are better than the manual laborers who cut and arrange the stones (and they are paid more); in the spiritual building the architects and planners are the bishops and teachers of theology, while parish priests are like the manual laborers. In his responses to the objections, St. Thomas points out that priests engaged in the active life have only an effect of perfection and are bound to the salvation of souls, while religious and bishops have the state of perfection and are bound only to their vows. We can only guess at the reaction of any members of the secular clergy in the audience during the discussion.

St. Thomas also came into conflict with certain Franciscans, e.g., John Pecham, and with the Dominican Robert Kilwardby over the number of substantial forms in a concrete individual. In general it was a conflict between a master who assimilated a good number of Aristotelian concepts into his metaphysics, and the opponents of such philosophical "innovations." In particular it was a disagreement as to whether an individual has only one substantial form, as St. Thomas (and Aristotle) maintained, or whether it has many, related to each other in a certain order. Kilwardby, for example, in his *Commentary on the Sentences* insisted that the constitution of an individual requires several forms in a single matter. Thus in one fire there is a form of fire, a form of body, and a form of substance. [33]

---

[32] Ibid.

[33] Étienne Gilson, *History of Christian Philosophy in the Middle Ages* (London, 1955), p. 357. For more on the background of the problem, see Daniel Callus, "The Origins of the Problem of the Unity of Form," *The Thomist* 24 (1961), 257-285.

St. Thomas took up this question at many points in his writings, including Quodlibet 1, q. 4, a.1; 11, q. 6; 12, q. 7, a.1; *Summa theologiae* 1, q. 76, arts. 3 and 4, and *Quaestiones de anima*, q. 11. In these last two works his position in favor of the unicity of substantial form is expounded in greater detail. In the *Summa*, for example, he offers three major arguments, only the first of which is sketched in the first Quodlibet. First there is the argument from unity. A thing with many substantial forms would not be absolutely one, because unity as well as being follows on substantial form. If there were many substantial forms, there would then be many beings in a thing and hence many unities. What would serve to bind these individual entities into one? St. Thomas apparently could find no answer; without such a binding factor, however, we do not have an individual substance but only an aggregate or heap which is one only in a relative sense.[34] But even with an aggregate we can separate out one stone, for example, from the others in a way that we cannot separate out the animal aspect of a man from the other constituents. Substantial form unites with matter as act with potency, and existence follows on the substantial form binding the whole, and any accidents added later, into one individual substance. There is no way for this binding or unification to occur among several actual substantial forms.

Second, there is the argument from predication, not used in the Quodlibets. Terms signifying aspects of a thing derived from the same form are predicated of each other *per se* in the first manner (i.e., the predicate is the definition of the subject, or part of it). Terms signifying aspects of a thing derived from diverse forms are predicated of each other only *per accidens*, or *per se* in the second manner (i.e., the subject is part of the definition of the predicate) when they are intrinsically related. If there is a plurality of substantial forms in a man then there will be a rational form, an animal form, a body form, etc. When we make a predication like "A man is an animal" then, the predication must be either *per accidens* or *per se* in the second manner. Now it cannot be accidental that a man is an animal, for "A man is an animal" says something about the human essence. The predication cannot be *per se* in the second manner, though, for 'animal' is part of the definition of 'man' and not conversely. The

---

[34] See *Quaestiones de anima*, q. 11, ed. J. H. Robb (Toronto, 1968), pp. 171-172.

predication must then be *per se* in the first manner, and thus a thing must be a man and an animal by one and the same form.

The third argument concerns the mutual hindrance of powers. When one activity of the soul is intense, we find that another may be hindered. For example, sensations are less intense when one is deep in thought. Now heat can hinder cold and water fire, but only because these are contraries and arise from diverse principles. Within a man, however, thought and sensation are not contraries, so it follows they must be rooted in one principle or substantial form.

There is actually a fourth argument used in *De spiritualibus creaturis*, q. 3, and in Quodlibets 11 and 12.[35] If there were many substantial forms, only the reception of the first would be generation in the proper sense. All the later forms would be accidental and hence not a part of the essence. Thus if the first substantial form is the vegetative, the sensitive and intellective which come later in the development of a human embryo would be accidental.

St. Thomas concludes that there is one substantial form only, and it makes a thing both exist and be one absolutely. When it arrives, any prior substantial form leaves. The more perfect the form the more it can accomplish, hence through one substantial form a thing can often perform activities associated with diverse forms – by the intellective soul a man can sense as the beasts do, nourish and grow like the plants, have a body, etc. According to him, the more perfect form virtually contains the less perfect – not as distinct essences in Kilwardby's fashion, but in the sense that it enables its bearer to do what the less perfect forms would enable it to do and still more. He frequently compares a perfect form containing the powers of less perfect forms to the relation of numbers or figures. The number five virtually contains the number four, a square virtually contains a triangle, and so on. If you have drawn a square and you then need a triangle, for many purposes you do not need to draw another figure – you can just divide the square into two triangles using one line. And so it is with the intellective soul which enables a human not only to reason but also to see, hear, remember, take nourishment, grow, reproduce, exist, etc. Yet we can distinguish rationality, sensitivity, and the other aspects as though they were really distinct.

---

[35] *De spiritualibus creaturis*, q. 3, ed. L. Keeler (Rome, 1946), p. 43.

That is simply because of the ways in which we compare man with other creatures. The distinction itself is a mental one only.

St. Thomas's doctrine arises out of an Aristotelian context in which matter is purely potential until given form, and form is purely act. Franciscans like Pecham or Bonaventure did not, however, share this background, and a doctrine of plurality of substantial forms did not present the difficulties for them it did for St. Thomas. For either Franciscan, matter need not be corporeal but can be spiritual, for matter is that in a thing which limits it.[36] There is then no difficulty in holding that the soul contains matter for it is indeed finite, it has potentialities. Soul is form with respect to the body, but it is not form simply. There can be only one substantial form when this form completely exhausts the potentiality of matter and the matter "absorbs" the activity of the form.[37] This is not so with soul and body. Neither has its potentialities exhausted by the other. This is true in other cases also. Unformed matter at the beginning of the world received the form of light which determined matter to exist but left open the kind of existence – matter thus had the potential to receive other substantial forms.[38] Form does not limit so much as it disposes a thing for other, higher perfections.[39]

The plurality of forms doctrine still leaves the problem of unification, however. This was felt by St. Bonaventure who nonetheless only suggested a solution.[40] John Duns Scotus was later to follow up on this suggestion with his formal distinction. According to him, it is not necessary to say that diverse substantial forms in a thing are really distinct and separable entities. There is a kind of real distinction which holds between formalities unitively contained within one thing.[41] However, this formal distinction in itself was to

---

[36] On John Pecham, see D. E. Sharp, *Franciscan Philosophy at Oxford in the Thirteenth Century* (London, 1930), pp. 185-203. On St. Bonaventure, see Efrem Bettoni, *St. Bonaventure*, trans. A. Gambatese (Notre Dame, 1964), pp. 83-87.

[37] Bettoni, *St. Bonaventure*, p. 85.

[38] Ibid., pp. 72-73.

[39] Frederick Copleston, *A History of Philosophy* (New York, 1962), vol. 2, part 1, pp. 304-305.

[40] See my article, "St. Bonaventure on Distinctions," *Franciscan Studies* 38 (1978), 194-212.

[41] John Duns Scotus, for example *Opus oxoniense* 2, d. 16, q. un., n. 17, and 4, d. 46, q. 3, n. 4; *Reportata parisiensia* 2, d. 15, q. un., etc., in *Opera omnia*, ed. L. Wadding (1639; reprint in 16 vols., Hildesheim: Olms, 1968). A thorough treatment of

generate as much controversy as the doctrine of the unicity of substantial form.

One reason the number of substantial forms became an issue is that if there is only one substantial form, then when a man dies the substantial form leaves and the body remaining is not truly the same as the body that lived before, although the matter and some of the accidents would remain, at least for a time. If there is no *forma corporeitatis* remaining the same in the living and the dead body after the rational soul departs, certain dangerous results follow, according to John Pecham:

> ... the resurrection of Christ or any miraculous restoration to life would have no meaning because the dead body would not be numerically and specifically identical with the original living one; what is common would be only the matter or the accidents and not the substantial form, the essential factor. With this, too, would fall the ground for the veneration of relics, since there would be no true identity between the relic and the living body. Again, if the persistence of the *forma corporeitatis* be denied, the Eucharistic doctrine would be undermined because the whole substance of bread is converted into the whole body of Christ and not only into its matter; ... Further, if a consecration occurred during the three days of Christ's death, the transubstantiation of the bread must have referred to the body into which a new specific form had been introduced.[42]

St. Thomas touches on this issue several times during the quodlibetal disputes (Quodlibet 4, q. 5; Quodlibet 3, q. 2, a.2) but his best treatment is to be found in Quodlibet 2, q. 1, a.1. In the case of an ordinary man, death is simply the separation of the soul, the substantial form of man, from the body. The concrete individual which was composed of both is then destroyed and only the material part remains. There is an identity of matter between the living body and the dead body, but there is diversity with regard to substantial form.[43] It is not proper to say that there is a man after death at all; rather, there is a dead man or a dead human body. The nature or essence, which consists of the essential principles, is destroyed when

---

the formal distinction is given by M. Grajewski in *The Formal Distinction of Duns Scotus* (Washington, D.C., 1944).

[42] Sharp, *Franciscan Philosophy at Oxford*, pp. 187-188.

[43] *Summa theologiae* 3, q. 50, a.5, ad 1, Blackfriars ed. (New York, 1964-1969), 54: 132-133.

the soul departs and with specific unity's loss there is a loss of numerical unity also.[44]

Christ truly died – a denial of this would involve one in the heresy of the Gaianites. Thus the soul or substantial form of Christ did separate from his body, for that is just what 'death' means. And, as St. Thomas's opponents objected, it would seem that with the removal of the form of the part there is loss of the form of the whole (i.e., humanity). Then Christ could not be the same man during the three days of death as he was before. There is no ground for the identity of the man Christ and the dead body of Christ.

In his response St. Thomas points out that there are three substances united in Christ – body, soul, and divinity. There is one nature constituted from body and soul, but divinity united to body and soul in the Person of the Word, i.e., in the supposit (though not in the nature for divinity remains distinct from humanity in the supposit). At death then, body and soul do separate, but divinity remains with each principle. Because of this identity, whatever is predicated of the body or the soul is predicated of the Son, e.g., he was buried because the body was, he descended into hell because the soul did.[45]

If we consider just the supposit, Christ was absolutely numerically the same after death because he was the same Person, the Son of God (though not of course the same human supposit). If we consider human nature, Christ was not the same man for the human nature was destroyed. If we consider the parts of human nature, the soul remained numerically the same after death; the body was numerically the same matter but the form was removed. Thus Christ was not absolutely numerically the same because the essence of the living body is life and that was lost. Nor was he absolutely other according to his whole substance, because the same matter remained.

There are difficulties with this position, however, and it is hard to see this reponse as satisfying St. Thomas's opponents. When the substantial form, the soul, departs from the body, it is presumably replaced by a distinct form of corporeity that makes that body a body simply. Then the body is not the same kind of thing it was before, a man – St. Thomas points out in Quodlibet 3, q. 2, a.2 that a dead man

[44] Ibid., ad 2.
[45] *Compendium theologiae*, c. 229, Leonine ed., vol. 42 (Rome, 1976).

can be called 'a man' only equivocally. Yet he often insists in his writings that numerical identity requires identity of both essential principles, matter and substantial form.[46] Christ remained the same supposit for the Word was still united to that body. But it was not a human body and so Christ could not have been the same man. The results of the union of the Word with a body that is not that of Christ the man may be peculiar in relation to the problems raised by John Pecham. At least in this case there is partial identity provided by the divinity's union with the body. In the case of ordinary men, however, there remains the problem of explaining the resurrection of the body in its essentials and its reunification with the soul which had informed it in this life.

Although it does not represent a particular controversy, Quodlibet 2, q. 2 is of interest because of the relation it bears to some of St. Thomas's most central metaphysical teachings. In the first article, "Whether an angel is composed of essence and being," there is a familiar argument establishing the distinction between these two principles in creatures. Unlike other versions of the argument, however, this one begins with a consideration of predications of the form 'A is φ'.[47] Such a predication can be essential, in which case 'φ' signifies the proper nature of A, or part of it. Thus 'Man is a rational mortal animal' is an essential predication, for being a rational mortal animal just is the essence of man. Or 'A is φ' can be a predication through participation when 'φ' signifies some characteristic in which A participates without having it totally. Such a predication can be rephrased usually as 'A has φ-ness,' as 'Socrates is white' can be rephrased as 'Socrates has whiteness.' If there were separated Platonic Forms (and St. Thomas does not think there are but supposes there are for the sake of making his point), each would have the totality of its nature and, where the subject terms signify such Forms and the predicates their natures, we could truly make such predications as 'Light is light,' 'Heat is hotness,' 'White is whiteness,' and so on.

---

[46] See, for example, *Summa contra gentiles* 4, c. 81, Leonine ed. (Rome, 1918-1930), 15: 252 and *Compendium theologiae*, c. 154, vol. 42.

[47] Other versions can be found in *De ente et essentia*, c. 5, ed. Boyer (Rome, 1970), pp. 39-40; *Summa contra gentiles* 2, c. 52, Leonine ed., 13: 387-388; *Scriptum super libros Sententiarum* 1, d. 8, q.4, a.3, ed. P. Mandonnet (Rome, 1930), 1: 222; ibid. 2, d. 1, q.1, a.1, same ed., 2: 12; and d. 3, q.1, a.1 and a.2, pp. 86-87.

These would be essential predications. There could be only one Form for each perfection for as he has shown elsewhere, a separated common nature can be only one.[48] Each would then embrace the totality of its nature. If individuals in the world have perfections like heat or light or whiteness, they can do so only by participation in such perfections. No individual has light or heat or whiteness in its totality. Rather, the nature in question is received by a limited thing like a rock or a man and is thus received according to the capacity of the recipient.[49]

This reasoning is then applied by St. Thomas to the case of being (*esse*). In predications such as 'A is' the meaning can be either 'A is being' and then the predication is essential, or 'A has being' and then there is predication through participation. As would be the case with a separated Form, there can be only one thing of which 'being' is predicated essentially, and that is subsistent being or *ipsum esse*.[50] Other things have being, participate in being, according to their capacities, but God alone is *ipsum esse*. What does the receiving must then be distinct from what it receives or participates in for it does not have that in totality. So the creature which has being also has an essence, and perhaps accidents as well, and is distinct from its being.

This, however, is not quite the essence-being distinction with which we are familiar, for St. Thomas has only established that a creature, not its essence, is distinct from its being. He now goes on to distinguish two ways in which 'A is φ' can be true when the predication is through participation. First it can be true when 'φ' signifies part of the substance or essence of A, e.g., when 'A' signifies a species and 'φ' the genus of that species as in 'Man is an animal.' Second it can be true when 'φ' does not signify something belonging to the essence, e.g., when it signifies an accident as in 'Socrates is white.' 'Being' is not predicated of a creature in the first way for it is not part of the definition signifying the essence of a thing.[51] Definitions consist of genus and difference and being cannot be a genus for if it were, as he shows in *Summa theologiae* 1, it could have

---

[48] *Summa contra gentiles* 2, c. 52 ; 13: 387-388; Quodlibet 3, a.8, ed. Spiazzi.

[49] *Summa contra gentiles* 1, c. 28, Leonine ed., 13: 86-87.

[50] For example, *De potentia*, q. 7, a.2, ad 5, Marietti ed., p. 192.

[51] See his earlier way of making the distinction between essence and being in *De ente et essentia* and *Scriptum super libros Sententiarum* (note 47 above).

no differences since a difference would already have to be in order to differentiate.[52] Being cannot be the whole definition either for that would consist of genus and difference together. 'Being' then must be predicated of a thing as something outside the thing's essence. This does not make it an accident, however, in the sense that qualities, quantities, and relation are accidents. It is predicated in a way analogous to the way in which an accident is predicated of a subject, but 'being' is predicated as the perfection par excellence while accidents are predicated as limited perfections.[53] Being follows on the reception of substantial form by matter and binds the two components together into one distinct existing individual. Without it, there can be no further perfections in a thing.

St. Thomas does not in this article take up the question of where being comes from. This has been done elsewhere, particularly in *De potentia*, q. 3 where he sketches three arguments.[54] First, what is common to many must be due to one cause for if each of the many were the cause, since they differ they would produce diverse effects instead of one. Being is common to distinct things and so must be due to some one cause. Second, when things participate in a perfection they do so by different degrees. But degrees can be attributed to them only in relation to some standard which they approach or fall away from. There must then be a perfect source of being and "It is necessary that all other less perfect things receive being from it." Third, what is through another is related to what is through itself as to a cause. One independent heat would cause heat in all hot things. There must then be one being which is its subsistent being (*ipsum suum esse*) and which causes being in all other things.

In earlier versions of the argument, St. Thomas sometimes made it appear that the distinction between essence and being was conceptual only. Thus in *De ente et essentia* we are told that an essence can be understood regardless of whether we know anything with that essence exists. We can understand what it is to be a phoenix, for example, without knowing whether there are any phoenixes.[55] Being is not part of the intelligible structure of any creature's essence. But

---

[52] *Summa theologiae* 1, q. 3, a.5, Blackfriars ed. (New York, 1964-1969), vol. 2.
[53] *De potentia*, q. 5, a.4, ad 3, Marietti ed., p. 139.
[54] Ibid., q. 3, a.5, and ad 1, pp. 48-49.
[55] *De ente et essentia*, ed. Boyer, pp. 39-40.

the development of the distinction in this article seems to indicate that it is a real one – not real in the sense of obtaining between separable individuals, but real in the sense of not being manufactured by the mind.[56] It is true that essence and being are really identical in any individual in the sense that they are principles of one supposit, but this is no bar to their being really distinct as principles of one thing, for substance and accident, matter and form, are really identical and really distinct in the same ways.[57] At least part of the purpose of the distinction is to establish a sharp contrast between God as subsistent being, or *ipsum esse*, and creatures which are composite to their very roots. Such a purpose could not be accomplished through a conceptual distinction alone.[58]

St. Thomas has now shown that a creature is not its existence, and that its essence is not its being. Is a creature the same as its essence then, or has he merely made the same point in two different ways? In the second article he addresses the related question "Whether supposit and nature are diverse in an angel?" After defining the terms 'supposit' and 'nature' St. .Thomas proceeds to refute the position that substantial form alone is nature or essence.[59] Definitions signify essence, and definitions of natural things include matter as well as form, for as he has said already in *De ente et essentia*, the genus is taken from matter and the difference from form, so matter is not included only accidentally. The definition must contain both components; so then must the essence. Some of his treatment of the

---

[56] For a discussion of the real nature of the distinction, see Joseph Owens, "Quiddity and Real Distinction in St. Thomas Aquinas," *Mediaeval Studies* 27 (1965), 1-22 and Joseph Bobik, *Aquinas on Being and Essence: A Translation and Interpretation* (Notre Dame, 1970), pp. 167-170.

[57] On types of identity and distinction, see my unpublished dissertation, *Medieval Theories of Distinction*, ch. 1, Philadelphia, Univ. of Penn., 1974.

[58] Some, for example, J. Owens, "Quiddity," see the argument as a proof for the existence of God. Others deny this, e.g., A. Maurer in his Introduction to his translation *On Being and Essence* (Toronto, 1968), pp. 19-27 (other sources are given in his footnote 35, p. 21). J. Deck, in "St. Thomas and the Language of Total Dependence," in *Aquinas: A Collection of Critical Essays*, ed. Anthony Kenny (New York, 1969), pp. 237-254, denies that the distinction can be used to establish the total dependence of creatures on God.

[59] An excellent discussion of the background of this refutation can be found in A. Maurer, "Form and Essence in the Philosophy of St. Thomas," *Mediaeval Studies* 13 (1951), 165-176.

question here parallels that of the above-mentioned work, which goes on to show that there are two ways to consider essences. First, the essence can be considered with precision from signate matter which individuates, and this is the abstract essence. Second, it can be considered without precision from signate matter, containing it implicitly and indistinctly, however, for signate matter as such is not subject to conceptualization or definition. This is the concrete essence. In the case of man, 'humanity' signifies the abstract essence, 'man' the concrete. Matter is included in the definition of the latter term as flesh and bones (though not *these* flesh and bones which belong to a particular individual man).[60]

An essence is subject to another threefold consideration. In Quodlibet 8, q. 1, a.1 we find the following passage, based on the *Metaphysica* of Avicenna:

> ... The consideration of any nature is threefold: with reference to the existence which it has in singular things, as the nature of a stone in this stone and in that stone; with reference to intelligible existence, as the nature of a stone is considered as it is in an intellect; absolutely, with reference to abstraction from both existences and in this way the nature of a stone or anything else is considered as far as concerns those aspects alone which are *per se* attributable to such a nature.[61]

Only the concrete essence can be predicated of individuals, for it is never correct to say 'Socrates is humanity' though we can correctly say 'Socrates is a man.'[62] 'Humanity' signifies the essence as a part, according to St. Thomas, leaving out all accidents and individuating principles which do belong to any individual like Socrates. 'Man' signifies as a whole, implicitly including such accidents and individuating principles. But it is only the concrete essence considered absolutely (and not as existing in individuals or in the mind) that is so predicable. An essence so considered abstracts from all existence, and consequently from all unity so there is no obstacle to its being identified with the individual in the manner required for predica-

---

[60] See *De ente et essentia* 3, ed. Boyer, p. 27; *Summa contra gentiles* 4, c. 81, Leonine ed., 15: 253; *Sententiae* 1, d. 23, q. 1, a.1, ed. P. Mandonnet (Rome, 1930), vol. 1; *Expositio in librum Boethii de hebdomadibus* 2, Marietti ed. (Taurino, 1954); *Compendium theologicae*, c. 154, Leonine ed., vol. 42.

[61] *Quaestiones quodlibetales*, ed. Spiazzi, p. 158. The translation is mine.

[62] See *De ente et essentia* 3, ed. Boyer, p. 27.

tion.[63] The individual, for example Socrates, is its essence in the sense that a definition of the essence gives the intelligible structure of the individual. What is omitted, the matter under quantitative dimensions, is not intelligible in itself so not definable. When we ask the question, 'What is Socrates?' we get the answer 'a man'. But we refer to 'the humanity of a man' as we would refer to 'the existence of a man' or 'the voice of a man', as a part of the individual.

The point of this article seems to go against what was just said, for here St. Thomas establishes that the individual and its essence are not identical. Yet if we consider the twofold division into abstract and concrete essence, it is true that the individual is distinct from its essence as abstract for Socrates is not humanity, nor even his humanity. The situation is similar to that for being – if there were a separately subsisting Form Man, it would be humanity. But in the case of creatures a nature like humanity is participated in; it is not the whole of the individual for there are accidents, signate matter, and being as well. Thus St. Thomas can say, "in the case of anything to which something which does not belong to the intelligible structure can be accidental, the thing and the essence, or the supposit and the nature, differ," when he means the abstract essence. 'White', 'Greek', 'bald', 'short', etc. all signify something apart from the abstract essence, but all are implicitly included in the notion of the concrete essence.[64]

Like the distinction between essence and being, that between abstract essence and individual is intended to be real. Once again St. Thomas makes a contrast with God in whom the divine essence is really identical with each of the supposits. Creatures are composite in a multitude of ways but God is entirely simple act. His essence is subsistent being and any supposit of that essence is the essence and is subsistent being.[65]

When St. Thomas deals specifically with angels here, he is in conflict with Franciscans like St. Bonaventure and John Pecham, and

[63] See In XII libros metaphysicorum expositio, ed. A. M. Pirrota (Taurino, 1948), book 7, 1365-1379. J. Owens discusses this identity in his "Common Nature: A Point of Comparison between Thomistic and Scotistic Metaphysics," in Inquiries into Medieval Philosophy, ed. J. Ross (Westport, Conn., 1971), pp. 193-194.

[64] In metaphysica, book 7, 1379.

[65] See also Summa theologiae 1, q. 3, a.3, Blackfriars ed., vol. 2; Sententiae 1, d. 34, q.1, a.1, ed. Mandonnet, vol. 1.

with Robert Kilwardby, who maintained a doctrine of universal hylomorphism according to which there is matter in every being except
God.[66] In the case of human souls and angels the matter is spiritual
rather than corporeal, but matter here simply represents potentiality.
So there can be many angels in a species individuated by their
matters. This position was not open to St. Thomas with his very
different conception of the role matter plays. Souls and angels can be
only forms. This does not equate them with God, however, for
articles 1 and 2 show that angels are composite in that in them
esse ̣ ce is distinct from being and from the supposit (in this case
a species rather than an individual).[67] Nonetheless this way of
regarding angels as species rather than individuals ran counter to the
thought of many theologians and was condemned along with some
other positions of St. Thomas in the Condemnations of 1277.

IV

The *Quaestiones quodlibetales* of St. Thomas occur in 137 manuscript
versions. The current standard printed editions are those found in the
Parma and Vives *Opera omnia*, the *Quaestiones quodlibetales* edited
by Spiazzi and published in Turin by Casa Marietti, and the edition of
Mandonnet published by Lethielleux. The Leonine Commission's
critical edition is still in preparation.

There has been no complete translation of the work into English,
although parts of some of the questions have appeared in various
anthologies of St. Thomas's works.[68] This translation of Quodlibets 1
and 2 is based on Spiazzi's edition which in turn is partly based on the
Parma version. I have compared it with the Vives version and made
corrections in either text where necessary.

---

[66] For the views of St. Bonaventure, John Pecham, and Robert Kilwardby, see
Gilson, *History of Christian Philosophy*, p. 339, pp. 204-205, and p. 357 respectively.

[67] See *Summa theologiae* 1, q. 3, a.3, Blackfriars ed., vol. 2; *Quaestiones de anima*,
q. 17, ad 10, ed. Robb; *In de anima* 3, 706, 710, Marietti ed. In these passages he seems
to contradict the position held in Quodlibet 2 that angels are distinct from their essences.

[68] *An Aquinas Reader*, ed. Mary T. Clark (New York, 1972); *The Pocket Aquinas*,
ed. Vernon J. Bourke (New York, 1965); *St. Thomas Aquinas Theological Texts*, ed.
Thomas Gilby (New York, 1955).

Citations of authorities are given in the text as they occur in Spiazzi and Vives. Where these are incorrect, the corrections have been made only in the corresponding footnotes. It should be noted that St. Thomas's quotations are often inaccurate in wording though I leave them unaltered for the inaccuracy in wording does not usually affect the sense. All translations from the authorities or from the Bible are my own. The Vulgate Bible has been used and where its numbering differs from that of more modern Bibles the Vulgate numbering has been included in parentheses.

The numbering of the articles in this translation corresponds to the numbering in Spiazzi's edition. Both the Vives and Parma editions give the articles consecutive numbers within each Quodlibet (i-xxii in Quodlibet 1, i-xvi in Quodlibet 2).

A bibliography of works on St. Thomas's *Quaestiones quodlibetales*, works referred to by St. Thomas, works of St. Thomas cited in footnotes or "parallel passages," and other works mentioned in the footnotes is included at the end.

St. Thomas Aquinas

Quodlibetal Questions 1 and 2

First Quodlibet

The question that has been asked is about God, both with regard to the divine nature and the human nature assumed.

QUESTION 1: The divine nature.

Article: Whether the blessed Benedict saw the divine essence in the vision in which he saw the whole world? [1]

And it was shown that he did.

1. For Gregory says in *Dialogorum* 2 where he speaks of this vision, that "All creation becomes insignificant for a soul that sees the Creator." [2] But to see God is to see the divine essence. Therefore, the blessed Benedict saw the divine essence.

2. Further, Gregory adds in the same place that "He saw the whole world in the divine light." [3] But there is no other light or radiance of God than God himself, as Gregory says and as the *Glossa* on Exodus 33:20, "No man will see me and live," says. [4] Therefore, the blessed Benedict saw God through the divine essence.

But to the contrary: John 1:18 says, "No man has seen God at any time." The *Glossa* says on this that "No one living in mortal flesh can see God's essence." [5]

---

[1] St. Benedict of Nursia, ca. 480-550, established the first monastic communities in the West and built the famous monastery at Monte Cassino where he wrote his Rule for religious life. See the article "St. Benedict" by J. Mallet in *The New Catholic Encyclopedia* (New York, 1967), vol. 2.

[2] Gregory the Great, *Dialogorum Libri IV*, 2, c. 35, ed. U. Moricca (Rome, 1924); PL 66: 200.

[3] Ibid.

[4] *Glossa ordinaria*, (Exod. 33), *Biblia sacra cum glossis ... Lyre* (No place, 1588), 1: 203; Gregory the Great, *Moralia* 18, c. 54; CC 143A: 953, no. 90, lines 97-98; PL. 76: 93.

[5] *Glossa ordinaria* (Iohannis Cap. 1), 5: 188b.

I answer: it must be said that, according to Wisdom 9:15, "A perishable body weighs the soul down." However, the highest elevation of the human mind is the attainment of a vision of the divine essence. So it is impossible for a human mind united to a body to see God's essence unless, as Augustine says in *Super Genesim ad litteram* 12, a man is entirely dead to this mortal life or is so separated from his senses that he does not know whether he is in or outside his body, as we read concerning Paul in 2 Cor. 12:3.[6] However, when he had that vision the blessed Benedict was neither entirely dead to this life nor separated from his bodily senses, which is clear from the fact that while remaining in the same vision he summoned another person to see the same thing, as Gregory relates. So it is clear that he did not see God's essence.

Therefore, to the first it must be said that Gregory means in those words to argue from a kind of proportion. For if the ones who see God's essence reckon all creation insignificant in comparison, it is not astonishing if the blessed Benedict could see something more through the divine light than men commonly see.

To the second it must be said that sometimes God himself is called the light of God, sometimes another light derived from God is called this, according to Psalm 36 (35):9, "In your light we shall see the light." Here, however, it means the light derived from God.

Parallel passage: st 2-2, q. 180, a.5, ad 3.

* * *

QUESTION 2: There were two points of inquiry concerning the human nature in Christ:
1. whether there is one sonship in Christ by which he is related to the Father and his mother, or two?
2. whether Christ was dead on the cross?

Article 1: Whether there is one sonship in Christ by which he is related to the Father and his mother, or two?

Concerning the first we proceeded as follows: it seems that there are two sonships in Christ.

---

[6] Augustine, *De Genesi ad litteram* 12, c. 27, ed. Jos. Zycha, csel. 28: 422; pl 34: 477-478.

1. For when the causes of relations are multiplied, the relations are multiplied. However, generation is the cause of sonship. Therefore since the generation by which Christ was born eternally from the Father and that by which he was born temporally from his mother are diverse, the sonship by which he is related to the Father and that by which he is related to his mother will also be diverse.

2. Moreover, what receives an absolute property in time without changing can even more receive a relative property in time without changing. But the Son of God receives an absolute property in time without changing because on Luke 1:32, "He shall be great and shall be called Son of the Highest," Ambrose says, "He will not therefore be great because he was not great before being born of the Virgin, but because the power which the Son of God has by nature the man was going to receive in time." [7] Therefore, even more could the Son of God receive a new sonship in time without changing. So two sonships are appropriate to him, one eternal and the other temporal.

But to the contrary: the unity of the cause which makes something such a thing makes it one such thing. But by sonship someone is a son, therefore by one sonship he is one son. Since Christ is one son and not two, there are not two sonships in him but one only.

I answer: it must be said that relations differ from all other categories of things in that those things which belong to other categories are real things from the very natures of their categories, as are quantities from the nature of quantity, and qualities fom the nature of quality.[8] But relations are not real things from the nature of relation.[9] For we find

---

[7] *Glossa ordinaria* (Lucae Cap. 1), 5, 125; attributed to Ambrose, *Expositio evangelii secundum Lucam*, though it does not occur in that work.

[8] The ten categories, outlined by Aristotle in his *Categoriae*, ch. 4 (*The Works of Aristotle*, ed. W. D. Ross [London, 1908-1952], vol. 1), are the most comprehensive genera or classes of things: substance, quantity, quality, relation, place, time, position, state, action, affection.

[9] According to St. Thomas (ST 1, q. 13, a.7, Blackfriars ed., vol. 3), when two terms are related to each other there are three possibilities. First, what we say of them may be true of them not because of anything real in each of them but because of how we think of them. This is the case with the terms of the simple identity relation and with the relation of a species to its genus. Second, what we say of them may be true because of something real in both terms, as is the case with the relations being-larger-than, being-changed-by, being-the-father-of, etc. Third, what we say of them may be true because of something real in one term but not in the other, especially when the terms belong to

certain relations which are not real but mental only, for example a knowable object is related to knowledge not by any real relation existing in the knowable object but rather because knowledge is related to the object, according to the Philosopher in *Metaphysica* 5.[10] But the reality of a relation comes from its cause when one thing has a natural order to another. The natural and real order is for them the relation itself. So right and left in an animal are real relations because they follow certain natural powers; however, in a column they are mental relations only according to an animal's position in relation to the column.

But a thing has being and unity from the same cause; and therefore, because of the unity of the cause it happens that there is only one real relation.[11] This is obvious in the case of equality, for there is in one body only one relation of equality because of the one quantity, although this may be in regard to a number of things insofar as it is said to be equal to different bodies. If relations were really multiplied in one body according to all those references to which it is equal, it would follow that there would be an infinite or in-determinate number of accidents in one thing. A teacher is by one relation a teacher of all whom he teaches the same thing although there may be many of these; so also according to one real sonship one man is the son of his father and of his mother because by one birth he received one nature from both of them. Therefore, following this reasoning, it seems that we must say that the real sonships in Christ by which he is related to the Father and to his mother are different because he is born from both by different acts of generation and the nature which he has from the Father and the nature which he has from his mother are diverse.

---

different orders. This is the case with the relation being-knowable-by for knowing an object is something real in the mind or senses of the knower though being knowable is not a reality in the object known. This is also the case with relations of creatures to God, as St. Thomas shows below. Relations of the first sort are mental while those of the second sort are real.

[10] Aristotle, *Metaphysica*, 5.15, 1021a29-35, *Works*, vol. 8.

[11] Being and unity are convertible, i.e., whenever something can be said to exist it can also be said to be one, and vice versa. Unity is undividedness according to St. Thomas, and something exists only so long as it is one. Thus the existence of a thing is grounded on its unity. See ST 1, q. 11, a.1, Blackfriars ed., vol. 2.

But another reason weakens that. For it must be universally held that no relation of God to creature really exists in God, but such is only a mental relation because God is above every order of creature and is the measure of every creature from which every creature derives, and not conversely. This is even truer of a knowable object in relation to knowledge, for in the knowable object there is no real relation to knowledge for these reasons.

We must, however, consider that the subject of sonship is not a nature or some part of a nature, for we do not say that humanity is a daughter nor that it is a head or an eye. Now in Christ we assign only one supposit and one hypostasis, just as we also assign one person which is an eternal supposit in which there can be no real relation to a creature as was just said.[12] So the only remaining alternative is that the sonship by which Christ is related to his mother is a mental relation only. But because of this it does not follow that he is not really the son of the Virgin, for just as God is really Lord because of the real power by which he contains a creature, so Christ really is the son of the Virgin because of the real nature which he received from his mother. If, however, there were many supposits in Christ it would be necesary to assign two sonships to Christ. But this I hold to be erroneous and it is found condemned in the Councils.[13] So I say that in Christ there is only one real relation by which he is related to the Father.

To the first it must therefore be stated that we do not deny there is a real sonship in Christ by which he is related to his mother because the relation's cause is lacking, but because the subject of such a relation is lacking, since there is no created supposit or hypostasis in Christ.

---

[12] 'Hypostasis' and 'supposit' both signify the concrete individual, a thing which exists on its own. 'Person' has the same meaning but in addition connotes that a rational being is being referred to. See sт 3, q. 16, a.2, ad 3, Blackfriars ed., 50: 46, and 3, q. 2, a.2, same ed., vol. 48.

[13] The error mentioned is one given serious consideration by Peter Lombard in 3 *Sent.*, d. 6, q.2, Quarrachi ed., 2: 574. It originated with Nestorius, patriarch of Constantinople 428-431, who held that the human body and soul united in Christ to make a man and that God dwelt in this man more than in others. There are thus really two persons, Christ who was God and Jesus who was man. Mary gave birth only to the latter who was the dwelling-place for the former. The position was condemned at the Council of Ephesus in 431. See cg 4, c. 34, Leonine ed., 15: 119, and John L. Murphy, *The General Councils of the Catholic Church* (Milwaukee, 1959), pp. 43-44.

To the second it must be stated that the same way in which that man received the power of God temporally, he received the eternal sonship inasmuch as it was accomplished in such a way that there would be one divine and human person, as Ambrose supposes in the same place. This, however, was not accomplished through something really absolute or relative temporally inhering in the Son of God, but solely through the union which really exists in the created nature but is not, however, really in the person assuming it.

What is objected on the contrary side has no necessity, for a thing is sometimes said to be one such thing because of the subject's substantial unity although there are many qualities in it, as there are color and taste in an apple.

Parallel passages: *Quodlibet* 9, q. 2, a.3; sт 3, q. 35, a.5; 3 *Sent.*, d. 8, q.1, a.4; *Comp. theol.*, c. 212.

Article 2: Whether Christ was dead on the cross?

Concerning the second we proceed as follows: it seems that Christ was not dead on the cross.

1. For if he was dead, this was either because he himself separated his soul from his body, or because of his wounds. But he did not die in the first way for then it would follow that the Jews would not have killed Christ but he would have killed himself, which is inappropriate. And likewise he did not die in the second way because a death due to wounds occurs when a man reaches the greatest weakness, which was not the case with Christ because he died crying out loudly. Therefore, Christ was in no way dead on the cross.

2. Moreover, human nature was no weaker in Christ than in other men, but no other man would die so quickly because of wounds of the hands and feet. The wound in the side, however, was inflicted on Christ after his death. Therefore, he was not dead on the cross since there seems to be no cause for his death.

But to the contrary: John 19:30 says that Christ hanging on the cross "with his head bowed, gave up the ghost." Death, however, is due to the soul's separation from the body, therefore Christ was dead on the cross.

I answer: it must be said that we must confess without any doubt that Christ was truly dead on the cross. In order to see the cause of his death we must consider that since Christ was true God and man, whatever pertains to Christ's human nature was subject to his power, which does not happen in others who are purely men for physical things are not subject to their wills. This is the cause of Christ's suffering and rejoicing simultaneously: by his willing, death was effected so that there would be no overflowing from the higher powers to the lower ones, nor would the higher powers be impeded in their own acts because of the suffering of the lower ones.[14] This cannot happen in other men because of the natural conjunction of the powers with one another.

And we must answer in like manner to that which was argued, for a violent death occurs because a nature yields to harm inflicted, and so long as the nature can resist so long is death delayed. Hence things in which a nature is stronger die more slowly from the same cause. However, how much the nature would resist harm inflicted and when it would yield were subject to Christ's will. Hence by his willing the nature resisted to the end the harm inflicted more than it could in other men so that in the end, after much effusion of blood and as though with his faculties still intact, he cried out with a loud voice, and at once by his willing the nature yielded and he gave up the ghost so that he might show himself Lord of nature and of life and death. And marveling at this, the centurion said in Mark 15:39, "Truly this man was the Son of God."

Therefore, it is true both that the Jews killed Christ by inflicting mortal harm, and that he himself laid down his soul and gave up the ghost because when he willed it his nature yielded totally to the harm inflicted. Nor is he to be blamed as though he killed himself. For the body exists for the sake of the soul and not conversely.[15] So injury is

---

[14] Christ's body suffered while his soul enjoyed the vision of God. He alone among men was able to prevent his higher part from affecting the lower; thus he could suffer in one part (the body), and not in the other (the soul). See *Compendium theologiae*, c. 230, Leonine ed., vol. 42.

[15] St. Thomas says the body exists for the sake of the soul and not conversely because the soul as a part of human nature is perfected only in union with a body. The soul, however, is capable of existence on its own since it has an operation, understanding, which transcends the body, though the material with which understanding operates is derived from objects in the physical world by means of sensation and imagination which utilize physical organs. St. Thomas regards the relation between soul and body as the relation between substantial form and matter. See CG 2, c. 68, Leonine

done to the soul when it is expelled from the body against the soul's
natural desire because of an injury inflicted on the body, although
perhaps not because of the depraved will of a suicide. But if the soul
had in its power the capacity to withdraw from and come into the
body again when it willed, there would be no greater blame if it
abandoned the body than if an inhabitant deserted a home. However,
it is a matter for blame for it to be expelled from thence unwillingly.

The response to the objections is clear.

Parallel passages: st 3, q. 47, a.1; *Comp. theol.*, c. 230; *In Ioann.*, c. 2.

* * *

Two questions were asked concerning angels.

QUESTION 3: 1. Whether an angel depends on a corporeal place
according to its essence or is it in a corporeal place
according to its action only?
2. Concerning an angel's motion, whether it can move
from one place to another without going through an
intermediate place?

Article 1: Whether an angel depends on a corporeal place according
to its essence, or is it in a corporeal place according to its
action only?

On the first we proceed as follows: it seems that an angel is not in a
place according to its action only.

1. For since existence is prior to action, existence in a place is prior
to action in a place. But something later is not the cause of something
prior. Therefore acting in a place is not the cause of an angel's existing
in a place.

2. Moreover, two angels can act in one place. Therefore, if an
angel were in a place only through action, it would follow that many
angels would exist simultaneously in one place, which is reputed to
be impossible.

---

ed., vol. 13: 440-441; st 1, q. 76, a.1, and a.5, Blackfriars ed., 11: 40-49, 72-74; *Quaest.
de anima*, q. 1, ed. Robb, p. 60; *De ente et essentia*, ed. Boyer, p. 45; *De spiritualibus
creaturis*, a.2, ad 5, ed. L. Keeler (Rome, 1946), p. 30, etc.

But to the contrary: something more noble does not depend on something less noble. But an angel's essence is nobler than a corporeal
place. Therefore, it does not depend on a corporeal place.

I answer: it must be said that we can consider the way an angel is in a
corporeal place from the way in which a body is in a place, for a body
is in a place through contact of the place. However, the contact of a
body is through dimensional quantity which is not found in an angel
since an angel is not physical but instead of it there is quantity of
power.[16] Therefore, just as a body is in a place through contact by
dimensional quantity, so an angel is in a place through contact by
power. If anyone wants to call contact by power an action because
action is properly the effect of a power, we may say that an angel is in
a place through action but in such a way that 'action' means not only
motion but any union by which its power unites itself to a body by
directing or containing it or in another way.

Therefore, to the first it must be stated that nothing prohibits
something from being absolutely prior which is not prior in this
respect. For example, a body is a subject absolutely prior to a surface,
but not as far as concerns color, and likewise a body is absolutely
prior to contact. However it is in a place through contact by
dimensional quantity. Similarly an angel is in a place through contact
by power.

To the second it must be stated that if something is completely
moved by one mover, it is not coherent that it be moved by another at
the same time. So the reasoning is more valid for its opposite rather
than for what is argued.

Parallel passages: st 1, q. 52, aa.1-3; De pot., q. 3, a.7, ad 11; a.19 ad 1 and 2;
    De sep. subs., c. 18, nos. 102-103; 1 Sent., d. 37, q.3, aa.1 and 3; 2
    Sent., d. 6, q.1, a.3.

---

[16] He defines dimensional quantity below (a.21) as "Quantity having position," and
in cg 4, c. 65, Leonine ed., 15: 209 as quantity which can be measured. By such
quantity a body is in a place as circumscribed by the place and commensurate with it (st
1, q. 52, a.2, Blackfriars ed., 9: 48; st 3, q. 76, a.5, Blackfriars ed., 58: 108). In contrast,
the contact of power which an angel has he defines as the power by which a thing is
touched insofar as it is acted upon and moved. By such contact an intellectual substance
can be united to a body. St. Thomas lists three characteristics: by means of such contact
an indivisible thing can touch a divisible thing; such contact relates to the whole thing
touched; such contact extends to the innermost thing, the toucher penetrating the thing
touched. See cg 2, c. 56, Leonine ed., 13: 403.

Article 2: Whether an angel can move from one place to another without passing through an intermediate place?

On the second we proceed as follows: it seems that an angel cannot move from place to place without passing through an intermediate place.

1. For everything that moves is in the process of changing before being in the state of completion of change, as *Physica* 6 proves.[17] But if an angel moves from one place to another, for example from A to B, when it is at B it is in the state of completion of change. Hence it was in the process of changing before. But not when it was at A because then it was not yet moving. Therefore, it will be in the process of changing when it is at C which is the intermediate between A and B. So it is necessary for it to pass through an intermediate.

2. Moreover, if an angel moves from A to B without passing through an intermediate, it will be necessary for it to be destroyed at A and created again at B. This is impossible because then it would not be the same angel. Therefore, it is necessary for it to pass through an intermediate.

But to the contrary: everything that passes through an intermediate must first pass through something equal to the thing or less before something greater, as is said in *Physica* 6 and as it appears to the senses.[18] But it cannot be less space than the angel which is indivisible, so it is necessary for it to pass through something equal to the angel which is an indivisible place like a point. An infinite number of points, however, lie between any two terms of motion. Therefore, if it were necessary for an angel in its motion to pass through an intermediate place, it would be necessary for it to pass through an infinite number, which is impossible.

I answer: it must be stated that an angel can if it wants move from one place to another without passing through an intermediate place, and if it wants it can pass through an intermediate place. The reason for this is that a body is in a place as contained by it, and therefore it is necessary that in moving it follow the condition of the place so that it passes through intermediate places prior to arriving at the boundaries of the place. But since an angel is in a place through contact by

---

[17] Aristotle, *Physica* 6.1, 231b25-232a17, *Works*, vol. 2.
[18] Ibid., 6.10, 241a6-10.

power, it is not subject to the place so as to be contained by it, but rather contains the place, being supereminent in the place by its power; so it is not necessary for it to follow the conditions of place in its motion. But it is subject to its will that it be attached to this place and that through contact by power, and without an intermediate place if it wants, just as an intellect can be attached to one extreme in understanding, e.g., to white, and afterwards to black, indifferently, either thinking or not thinking of the colors in between (although a body subject to color cannot move from white to black except through an intermediate color).

To the first it must therefore be stated that the Philosopher's words and his proof concern continuous motion. However, an angel's motion is not necessarily continuous, but we call the very succession of the aforesaid applications its motion, just as we call the succession of thoughts or states of mind the motion of a spiritual creature according to Augustine in *Super Genesim ad litteram*.[19]

To the second it must be said that this does not happen through the destruction or new creation of an angel, but because its power is supereminent over a place.

As to what is objected on the contrary side, it must be said that an angel is not in a place through having a common measure with the place but through the application of its power to the place, which application can indifferently be to a divisible and to an indivisible place. So it can move continuously as something which exists in a divisible place by continually intercepting space. But according as it is in an indivisible place its motion cannot be continuous nor pass through all intermediates.

Parallel passages: ST 1, q. 53, a.2; 1 *Sent.*, d. 37, q.4, a.2.

Then it was asked concerning man: first as to the good in the order of nature, second as to the good in the order of grace, third as to the good in the order of glory.

* * *

QUESTION 4: Three questions were asked about the good in the order
         of nature:

---

[19] Augustine, *De Genesi ad litteram* 8, c. 20; CSEL 28: 259; PL 34: 388.

1. concerning the union of soul and body, whether
when the soul arrives at the body all the forms
which inhered in the body before, both substantial
and accidental ones, are destroyed?
2. concerning the power of free choice, whether a man
without grace can prepare himself for grace?
3. concerning natural love, whether man in the state of
innocence loved God more than all things and above
himself?

Article 1: Whether when the soul arrives at the body all the forms
which inhered in the body before, both substantial and
accidental ones, are destroyed?

On the first we proceeded as follows: it seems that all the forms which
inhered before are not removed through the arrival of the soul.

1. For Genesis 2:7 says, "God formed man from the mud of the
earth and breathed into his face the breath of life." However, the body
would have been formed uselessly if, in breathing in the soul, the
forms which he had imparted in giving form to it were removed.
Therefore, when the soul arrives, all the preceding forms are not
removed.

2. Moreover, the soul necessarily exists in a body endowed with
form and having many dispositions. If therefore the arriving soul
removes all the preceding forms and dispositions, it follows that in an
instant the soul gives form to the whole body. But it seems God alone
can do this.

3. Further, the soul exists only in a heterogeneous body. But a
mixture of elements involves the forms and not only the matter of the
elements, otherwise there would be destruction and not mixture.
Therefore, the soul does not remove all the forms found in matter.

4. Further, the soul is a perfection. Now a perfection does not
destroy, rather it perfects. Therefore, in arriving at the body it does
not destroy the pre-existing forms.

But to the contrary: every form which arrives at something actually
existent is accidental, for a substantial form makes actual being (*esse*)
absolutely. But if an arriving soul did not destroy the pre-existing
forms but was added on to them, it would follow that it would arrive
at an actually existing thing because any form, since it is an act,

makes actual being. Therefore, the arriving soul removes the pre-existing forms.

I answer: it must be stated that it is impossible for there to be many substantial forms in one and the same thing because a thing has its being and unity from the same source.[20] It is clear, however, that a thing has being through form, hence it also has unity through form. And because of this, wherever there is a multitude of forms there is not one thing absolutely, just as a white man is not one absolutely nor would a biped animal be one absolutely if it were an animal from one component and biped from another, as the Philosopher says. But substantial forms are related to one another as numbers are, as is said in *Metaphysica* 8, or as figures are as the Philosopher says concerning the parts of the soul in *De anima* 2.[21] For always the greater number or figure virtually contains in itself the lesser as five contains four and as a pentagon contains a figure with four sides. And similarly the more perfect form virtually contains in itself the more imperfect as is most clear in the case of animals. For the intellective soul has the power to confer on the human body whatever the sensitive soul confers in brute animals, and likewise the sensitive does in animals whatever the nutritive does in plants, and still more. Therefore, in man another sensitive soul in addition to the intellective soul would be useless because the intellective virtually contains the sensitive and still more, just as, given that you have something containing five members, it would be useless to add something containing four. And there is the same reasoning for all substantial forms down to prime matter so that diverse substantial forms are not found in a man except to our way of thinking, as when we consider him as living by means of a nutritive soul and as sensing by means of a sensitive soul, and so on concerning the others.

Clearly, however, when a perfect form arrives an imperfect form is always removed. For example, when the figure of a pentagon arrives

---

[20] The doctrine of unicity of substantial form adopted by St. Thomas was opposed to the doctrine of plurality of substantial forms derived originally from Avicebron (Ibn Gabirol) in his *Fons vitae*, 2.3, ed. C. Baeumker, *BGPMA* (Münster, 1892-1895), Band 1, Heft 1, p. 28 (also 3, 23, p. 133 and 26, p. 142), and adopted by the Dominican Robert Kilwardby and many Franciscans. See the Introduction, pp. 12-18 above, for more on the conflict between the two doctrines.

[21] Aristotle, *Metaphysica*, 8.3, 1043b33-1044a14, *Works*, vol. 8; *De anima*, 2.3, 414b20-415a1, *Works*, vol. 3.

that of a rectangle is removed. So I say that when the human soul arrives, the substantial form which inhered before is removed. Otherwise there would be generation of the one without the destruction of the other which is impossible. The accidental forms which inhered before and prepared for the soul are not indeed destroyed essentially but accidentally when the subject is destroyed. So they remain specifically but not numerically the same, as also happens concerning the dispositions of the forms of the elements which seem to reach matter first.

To the first it must be stated therefore that according to Basil, the grace of the Holy Spirit is there called the breath of life, and so the objection ceases.[22] However, if as Augustine says the breath of life is the soul itself, it will not be necessary to say that the human body is given form from the mud of the earth with a form other than the very breath of life divinely breathed in.[23] For that imparting of form did not precede in time the breathing-in, unless perhaps we should want to say that the imparting of form is referred to the accidental dispositions, e.g., shape and the like, which by a certain order of reason are understood to be in the body as material dispositions before the intellective soul arrives. But the intellective soul is itself presupposed by these dispositions, not as intellective but as containing in itself virtually something of the more imperfect forms.

To the second it must be said that the soul, when it arrives at the body, is not the efficient but only the formal cause of the body's being.[24] However, that which is the efficient cause of the body's form makes the body to be as perfecting it; that which works beforehand on the form by gradually and in a certain order bringing matter to a closer form or disposition makes the body to be by preparing it. The nearer a form or disposition is, the less the resistance to the introduction of the form and complete disposition. For fire is more

---

[22] Basil, perhaps *Contra Eunomium* 5, PG 29: 728.

[23] Augustine, *De civitate Dei* 12, c. 24, ed. B. Dombart and A. Kalb CC 48: 381 (Turnholti, 1955); CSEL 40: 608; PL 41: 373.

[24] Aristotle posited four types of cause, two of which are mentioned by St. Thomas here. The matter and form of a thing constitute its material and formal causes. They are intrinsic to a thing. The efficient cause is the moving cause and there is also a final cause, the end or goal of a process. See *De principiis naturae* 3, Leonine ed. (Rome, 1976), vol. 43, and *Metaphysica* 5, lect. 2, Marietti ed.

easily made from air than from water, although each form is immediately present in matter.

To the third it must be said that Avicenna maintained the forms of the elements remain in a mixture in act.[25] This cannot be because the forms of the elements cannot exist in one and the same part of matter at the same time, and so it is necessary that they exist in diverse parts of matter which are distinguished according to the division of dimensional quantity. Then it will be necessary that either many bodies exist at the same time or that it is not a true mixture of every part to every part but a mixture appearing to the senses only, because of the juxtaposition of the smallest particles. Averroes, however, in *De caelo* 3, says that the forms of the elements are intermediate between accidental and substantial forms, and that they receive degrees of more and less.[26] And so, when the forms of the elements are modified and reduced to equilibrium, somehow a mixture is made. But this is less possible than the first opinion. For a substantial form is a kind of limit to specific existence whence in an indivisible the notion of form is like the notion of number and shape, nor is it possible that it be more intense or less, but every addition or subtraction makes another species. And therefore we must say otherwise, following the Philosopher in *De generatione* 1, that the forms of the components do not remain in the mixture actually, but they remain virtually according as the power of the substantial form remains in the elementary quality although modified and reduced as it were to equilibrium.[27] For an elementary quality acts in virtue of a substantial form. Otherwise the action which is through the heat of fire would not be terminated in a substantial form.

To the fourth it must be stated that the soul, since it is a form, is indeed a kind of particular perfection, however not a universal one. And therefore when it arrives something is perfected but in such a way that something else is destroyed.

Parallel passages: Quodlibet 11, q. 5; sT 1, q. 76, a.4; 4 *Sent.*, d. 44, q.1, a.1, qc 1, ad 4; cG 4, c. 81; *Spir. creat.*, a.3; *Quaest. de anima*, q. 9; *Comp. theol.*, c. 90.

---

[25] Avicenna, *Sufficientia* 1, c. 6, *Opera*, vol. 2; *Avicenna Latinus: Liber de anima*, ed. S. Van Riet (Leiden, 1968), P. 4, c.5, *Opera*, vol. 5.

[26] Averroes, *De caelo* 3, Comm. 67, *Opera* 5: 105r.

[27] Aristotle, *De generatione et corruptione* 1, 10, 327b23-27, *Works*, vol. 2.

Article 2: Whether a man without grace can prepare himself for grace?

On the second we proceeded as follows: it seems that a man without grace can prepare himself for grace through the natural liberty of choice.

1. Because as Proverbs 16:1 says, "To prepare the mind pertains to man." However, that is said to pertain to someone which is assigned to his power. Therefore, to be able to prepare himself for grace was assigned to the power of man. He does not then need the aid of grace.

2. Moreover, Anselm says in *De casu diaboli* that someone does not lack grace because God does not want to give it but because he does not want to receive it.[28] Therefore, if he wanted to receive it he could, so he can if he wants prepare himself for grace without external aid.

3. But the objector said that a man needs the aid of grace in this matter as an external mover. On the contrary: we can say that a man can be moved to conversion not only from good things but even from sins, for example if someone should see someone sinning heinously and from the horror of the sin be turned to God. But the sin is not from God. Therefore, without God's action a man can prepare himself for grace.

But to the contrary: we are prepared for grace through being turned to God. But for this we need the aid of divine grace for Lamentations 5:21 says, "Convert us, Lord, to you, and we shall be converted." Therefore, to prepare himself for grace a man needs the aid of divine grace.

Moreover, a man cannot prepare himself for anything except by thinking. But for this itself a man needs the aid of grace, for it is said in 2 Cor. 3:5, "We are insufficient of ourselves to think anything as from ourselves." Therefore, we need the aid of divine grace to prepare ourselves for grace.

I answer: it must be said that in this question we must guard against the error of Pelagius who maintained that through free choice a man could fulfill the law and merit eternal life nor needed divine aid except in order to know what to do, according to Psalm 143 (142):10,

---

[28] Anselm, *Dialogus de casu diaboli* 3, PL 158: 329; ed. F. S. Schmitt (Edinburgh, 1946-1961), 1: 240.

"Teach me to do your will." [29] But because this seemed much too little (for then we would have knowledge only from God but the charity by which the precepts of the law are fulfilled we would have from ourselves), the Pelagians afterwards maintained that a man has the beginning of a good work from himself when he consents to faith through free choice, but a man has the consummation of the work from God. But preparation pertains to the beginning of a good work. So saying that a man may be able to prepare himself for grace without the aid of divine grace pertains to the Pelagians' error and is against the Apostle who says in Phil. 1:6, "He who has begun a good work in you will perfect it."

Therefore, a man needs the aid of grace not only to merit but even to prepare himself for grace, but in different ways. For a man merits through an act of virtue when he not only does good but does well, for which a habit is required as is said in *Ethica* 2.[30] And therefore, grace in the mode of a habit is required for meriting. But for a man to prepare himself to acquire a habit he does not need another habit because then the process would go on to infinity. However, he needs divine aid not only with regard to exterior movers insofar as divine providence procures for a man occasions for salvation, e.g., teaching, examples, and occasionally sicknesses and tribulations, but even with regard to interior motion insofar as God moves the interior heart of a man to the good, according to Proverbs 21:1, "The heart of the king is in the hand of God; he will turn that wherever he wants." That this is necessary the Philosopher proves in a chapter of *De bono fortunae*, for a man does this by his will; however, the principle of the will is choice and of choice, counsel.[31] But if it were asked what kind of counsel he should begin to take, it cannot be said that he should begin to take counsel from a counsel because thus the process would be infinite. So it is necesary for there to be some exterior principle which moves the human mind to taking counsel concerning things to be done, and this must be something better than the human mind. Hence it is not a celestial body which is lower than an intellectual power, but God, as the Philosopher concludes in the same place. Therefore, just

---

[29] On the beliefs of Pelagius, see Augustine, *De haeresibus*, ed. M. van den Hont et al. cc 46: 340-342 (Turnholti, 1969); PL 42: 47-48.

[30] Aristotle, *Ethica nicomachea* 2.6, 1106a15-1106b28, *Works*, vol. 9.

[31] Aristotle, *Ethica eudemia* 2, *Works*, vol. 9.

as the principle of every motion of lower bodies which are not always moved is the motion of the heavens, so the principle of all interior motions of minds is God as mover.[32] No one then can prepare himself for grace nor do anything good except through divine aid.

Therefore, to the first it must be stated that the necessity of divine aid is not excluded because it pertains to a man to prepare himself for grace through free choice, just as neither is the necessity of heavenly motion excluded because it pertains to fire to heat.

To the second it must be stated that God moves everything according to its manner. So divine motion is imparted to some things with necessity; however, it is imparted to the rational nature with liberty because the rational power is related to opposites. God so moves the human mind to the good, however, that a man can resist this motion. And so, that a man should prepare himself for grace is from God, but that he should lack grace does not have its cause from God but from the man, according to Hosea 13:9, "Your ruin is from youself, Israel; your help is only from me."

To the third it must be stated that although sin is not from God, God sometimes arranges sin to be the occasion of someone's salvation.

Parallel passages: ST 1, q. 62, a.2; 1-2, q. 109, a.6; 2 *Sent.*, d. 5, q.2, a.1; d. 28, q.1, a.4; 4, d. 17, q.1, a.2, qc 2 ad 2; CG 3, c. 149; *De ver.*, q. 24, a.15; *In Ioann.*, c. 1, lect. 6; *Ad Hebr.*, c. 12, lect. 3.

Article 3: Whether man in the state of innocence loved God above all things?

On the third we proceed as follows: it seems that the first man in the state of innocence did not love God above all things and more than himself.

1. For so to love God is most meritorious. But the first man in that state did not have that whereby he might be able to advance by means of merit, as is said in *Sententiarum* 2, d. 24.[33] Therefore, the first man in that state did not love God more than himself and above all things.

2. Further, so to love God is the human mind's greatest preparation for attaining grace. However, the first man in that state is

---

[32] See CG 3, c. 82, Leonine ed., 14: 243-244 on the movement of lower bodies by the heavenly bodies.

[33] Peter Lombard, *Sententiae* 2, d. 24, c.1, Quaracchi 1: 419; PL 192: 701-702.

held not to have had grace but only natural endowments. Therefore, he did not love God more than himself and above all things.

3. Moreover, nature curves back upon itself, since it channels back to itself all things that it loves. But the adequate cause of each thing is of like kind only more so. Therefore, by natural love he loved himself more than God so he did not love God above all things.

But to the contrary: if he did not love God more than himself, either he loved him less than himself or equally with himself. In each way it follows that man took pleasure in himself while he did not refer himself to God. However, taking pleasure in oneself brings the perversity of sin, as Augustine says.[34] Therefore, the first man in the state of innocence was already perverted through sin, which is impossible. So it follows that he loved God above all things.

I answer: it must be said that if man was made in grace, as can be seen from the words of Basil and Augustine, the question is pointless.[35] For it is clear that someone who is in a state of grace loves God through charity above himself. But because it was possible for God to make man with purely natural endowments, it is useful to consider how much natural love could be extended.

Some said that a man or an angel existing in a purely natural state loves God more than himself by a natural love according to the love of desire, because he desires more the enjoyment of the divine good as something higher and sweeter.[36] But a man naturally loves himself more than God according to the love of friendship.[37] It is by the love of desire that we are said to love that which we want to use or enjoy, such as wine or some such thing; however, the love of friendship is that by which we are said to love a friend to whom we wish good.

---

[34] Augustine, *De civitate Dei* 14, cc. 12, 13; CSEL 40: 30-33; CC 48: 433-436; PL 41: 420-422.

[35] Basil, *Contra Eunomium* 5, PG 29: 728; Augustine, *De gratia Christi* 2, c. 13, ed. Urba and Zycha; CSEL 42: 176; PL 44: 391; *De gestis Pelag.*, c. 10, no. 22; CSEL 42: 75; PL 44: 333; and *De civitate Dei* 13, c. 13, CSEL 40: 631; CC 48: 395; PL 41: 386.

[36] He may be referring to Albert the Great, *Sent.* 2, d. 3, q. 18, ed. A. Borgnet, *Opera* 27: 98, and William of Auxerre, *Summa aurea in quattuor libros sententiarum* (Paris, 1500; rept. Frankfurt a.M., 1964), 2, tr. 1, c. 4.

[37] The love of friendship (*amor amicitiae*) is that in which the object is loved simply and of itself. The love of desire (*amor concupiscentiae*) is that in which the object is loved for something besides itself. See also ST 1-2, q. 26, a. 4, Blackfriars ed., 19: 71-73.

This position cannot stand, for natural love is a kind of natural inclination engrafted in a nature by God. But nothing natural is perverse, therefore it is impossible for any natural inclination or love to be perverse. Since it is a perverse love for someone to love himself more than God by the love of friendship, such a love cannot be natural. So we must say that to love God above all things and more than oneself is natural not only for an angel and a man but also for any creature according as it can love sensitively and naturally for natural inclinations can especially be known in these things which are done naturally without the deliberation of reason, for in this way everything in nature is born to act as is fitting. But we see that any part, by a kind of natural inclination, works for the good of the whole, even to its own danger or detriment, for example when someone exposes his hand to a sword to defend his head on which his whole body's health depends. So it is natural that any part in its way loves the whole more than itself. And also according to this natural inclination and according to political virtue, the good citizen faces the danger of death for the common good. But it is clear that God is the common good of the whole universe and of all its parts, so any creature in its way naturally loves God more than itself — insensible things do so naturally, brute animals sensitively, rational creatures through the intellectual love which is called love (*dilectio*).[38]

To the first it must therefore be said that to love God as the principle of all being pertains to natural love, but to love God as the object of beatitude pertains to the gratuitous love in which merit consists. However, it is not necessary that we sustain in this matter the opinion of the Master who said that man in the first state did not have the grace through which he could merit.

To the second it must be said that someone can make more or less use of the natural love by which God is naturally loved above all things, and when he uses it in the highest way there is the supreme preparation for having grace.

---

[38] In general St. Thomas distinguishes three types of love. *Amor* is love which pertains to the appetites — natural, sensitive, or intellectual. *Dilectio* adds to the notion of *amor* the notion of a preceding choice so that this type of love cannot be found in the concupiscible appetite but must belong to the will of a rational being. *Caritas* adds to these notions that of a kind of perfection of love, the object of love being esteemed as something of great value. See ST 1-2, q. 26, a.3, Blackfriars ed., 19: 68-71.

To the third it must be said that the natural inclination of a thing is to two things: to motion and to action. Now that natural inclination to motion curves back on itself just as fire moves upwards for the sake of its conservation, but that natural inclination to action does not curve back on itself, for fire does not act to generate fire for its own sake but for the good of what is generated which is its form, and further for the common good which is the conservation of the species. Hence it is clear that it is not universally true that every natural love curves back on itself.

Parallel passages: ST 1, q. 60, a.5; 1-2, q. 109, a.3; 2-2, q. 26, a.3; 2 *Sent.*, d. 3, p.2, q.3; 3, d. 29, a.3; *De div. nom.*, c. 4, lects. 9, 10.

* * *

Then the question was asked concerning matters which pertain to the good in the order of grace: first, concerning these matters which pertain to the good in the order of grace itself; second, concerning these matters which pertain to the evil of sin which is opposed to it. Concerning those matters which pertain to everyone, the question was asked about two parts of penance: [39]

1. concerning contrition, whether namely a contrite person ought to prefer being in hell to sinning?
2. concerning confession.

QUESTION 5: Concerning contrition.

Article: Whether a contrite person ought to prefer being in hell to sinning?

On the first we proceeded as follows: it seems that a contrite person ought not to prefer being in hell to sinning.

1. For the punishment of hell is eternal and irremediable, but he can be freed from sin through repentance. Therefore, he ought to prefer sinning to being in hell.

2. Further, the punishment of hell includes guilt, for one of the punishments of hell is the worm, i.e., remorse of conscience concern-

---

[39] Contrition and confession are two of the three parts of penance. The third is satisfaction. In contrition the mind turns to God and away from sin, grieves for its sins, and proposes not to sin again. In contrition the mind is reordered to God. In confession a fault is made known to a priest so that it can be judged. In satisfaction the penalty due for the sin is paid and one is then freed from the guilt of punishment. See ST 3, q. 90, a.1, Blackfriars ed., 60: 162-163, and CG 4, c. 72, Leonine ed., 15: 225-226.

ing a sin, but guilt does not include the punishment of hell. Therefore, sin is to be preferred to the punishment of hell.

But to the contrary: Anselm says in *De similitudinibus* that someone ought to prefer being in hell without sin to being in paradise with sin, because an innocent person in hell would not feel the punishment and a sinner in paradise would not enjoy the glory.[40]

I answer: it must be said that in general, a contrite person is bound to prefer suffering any punishment to sinning because there can be no contrition without the charity through which all sins are renounced. From charity a man loves God more than himself, but sinning is acting against God. Now to be punished is to suffer something against oneself. So charity requires that a contrite person prefer any punishment to guilt.[41]

But in a particular case he is not bound to descend to a consideration of this or that punishment. Rather someone would act foolishly if he were to worry himself or another over such particular punishments, for it is clear that just as desirable things move one more when considered in particular than when considered in general, so do terrible things frighten more if considered in particular. And there are some people who do not fall to a lesser temptation who would perhaps fall to a greater one, e.g., somone who just hears of adultery is not incited to lust but if in thought he descended to considering particular allurements he would be moved more. Likewise someone might not run away from undergoing death for Christ, but if he were to descend to considering individual punishments he would be more restrained from doing it. And therefore, to descend to a consideration of such particulars is to lead a man to temptation and to supply an occasion for sinning.

Therefore, it must be said to the first that deadly guilt is also of itself perpetual, but it can be cured by God's mercy alone. Moreover, the divine good against which guilt acts more outweighs the good of a created nature to which the punishment is opposed than the perpetuity of the punishment outweighs the temporality of guilt.

---

[40] Eadmer, *Liber de sancti Anselmi similitudinibus*, PL 159: 701.

[41] Charity is love of God for his own sake, and love of other creatures which are capable of attaining beatitude, i.e., rational creatures. It resists every hindrance so that it cannot exist with mortal sin which is an obstacle to beatitude. See *De caritate* 2, ed. E. Odetto (Taurino, 1953), Marietti ed.

To the second it must be said that remorse of conscience is not guilt but the consequent of guilt and could arise without guilt as in the case of one who has an erring conscience from a past act of commission, e.g., if someone believes some act he committed before was unlawful when, however, it was permissible and he himself reckoned it permissible while he committed it.

Parallel passages: 4 *Sent.*, d. 17, q.2, a.3, sol. 1, ad 4; *Suppl.*, q. 3, a.1, ad 4; *In Ps.*, 37.

* * *

QUESTION 6: Then three questions were asked about confession:
1. whether it is sufficient for someone to confess in writing, or is it necessary for him to confess by spoken word?
2. whether someone is bound to confess immediately when there is opportunity or can he wait till Lent?
3. whether a parish priest ought to believe his subject when he says he confessed to another priest and give him the Eucharist?

Article 1: Whether it is sufficient for someone to confess in writing or is it necessary for him to confess by spoken word?

On the first we proceeded as follows: it seems that it is sufficient for someone to confess in writing, for confession is required for the manifestation of a sin, but a sin can be manifested in writing as well as by spoken word. Therefore, it suffices if he confesses in writing.

But to the contrary: in Romans 10:10 it is said, "Confession is made orally for salvation."

I answer: it must be said that confession is part of a sacrament. So just as in baptism something is required on the minister's part, namely that he cleanse and speak the words, and something on the part of the one submitting to the sacrament, namely that he intend to and be cleansed, so in the sacrament of penance it is required on the priest's part that he absolve under some form of words, on the penitent's part it is required that he subject himself to the keys of the Church, manifesting his sins through confession. Therefore, it is essential to the sacrament that he manifest his sins, and no one may dispense from this as neither may anyone dispense from baptism. But it is not essential to the sacrament that the manifestation be made by spoken word, otherwise no one could receive the effect of this sacrament in any case of necessity except by confessing orally, which is clearly false for it is sufficient for mutes or anyone who cannot confess orally to confess by writing or gestures. However, in no case of necessity can anyone be baptized except by water because water is essential to the sacrament.

But from the Church's decree a man who can is bound to confess by spoken word, not only because the one confessing orally blushes more in confessing so that he who sins orally is cleansed orally, but also because in all the sacraments that whose use is more common is always accepted. So in the sacramental cleansing of baptism, water, which men more commonly use to wash with, is accepted, and in the Eucharist bread, which is a rather common food, and so also in the manifestation of sins it is fitting to use spoken words by which men are more commonly and with more clarity accustomed to signify their concepts.

And in this sacrament a character is not imprinted, but grace for the remission of sin alone is conferred, which no one obtains by sinning. However, he who ignores the Church's decrees sins; so in baptism he who preserves what is essential to the sacrament while overlooking the laws of the Church obtains the character of the sacrament but here, however, nothing follows.

However, the reasons which are introduced for both sides are not very compelling. For manifestation of sins cannot be so expressly done in writing as in spoken words, nor is what is said in "Confession is made orally for salvation" meant with regard to the confession of sins but rather with regard to the confession of faith.

Parallel passage: *Suppl.*, q. 9, a.3.

Article 2: Whether someone is bound to confess immediately when there is opportunity or can he wait till Lent?

Concerning the second we proceed as follows: it seems that someone can delay confession until Lent.

1. For whoever keeps the teaching of the Church is not delinquent. But the Church established that men should confess their own sins once a year. Therefore, if someone waits till the term established by the Church he does not sin.

2. Moreover, baptism is a sacrament of necessity as penance is also. But a catechumen does not sin if he delays baptism until Holy

Saturday. Therefore, for the same reason neither does a contrite person sin if he delays confession until Lent.

3. Further, contrition is more necessary than confession. But confession without contrition is not strong enough for salvation, though contrition without confession can be strong enough in some cases. Now he who is in sin is not bound to be penitent immediately by the contrition which abolishes sin, otherwise the sinner would sin in every single moment. Therefore, neither is the contrite person bound to confess immediately with the result that if he does otherwise he sins.

But to the contrary: a spiritual disease is more to be relieved than a physical disease. But someone subject to a physical disease would endanger himself unless he sought the remedy of medicine as quickly as he could, and he would sin from negligence. Therefore, all the more does he sin who delays to apply the remedy of confession against the spiritual disease of sin.

I answer: it must be said that it is laudable for the sinner to confess his sin as quickly as he conveniently can because a grace is conferred through the sacrament of penance which makes a man stronger in resisting sin. However, some said that he is bound to confess as quickly as the opportunity of confessing offered itself so that if he delays he sins. This is against the intelligible structure of an affirmative precept which, although it obliges always, does not however oblige for always but obliges for a fixed place and time. Now the time for fulfilling the precept concerning confession is when an occasion is imminent in which it is necessary for a man to confess, e.g., if the moment of death is imminent, or the necessity of receiving the Eucharist or Holy Orders or the like, for which it is necessary for a man to be prepared by being cleansed through confession. So if one of these events is imminent and someone neglects confession, he sins as long as a due opportunity is present. And because from the Church's precept all believers are bound to take the communion of the sacrament at least once a year, on the feast of Easter especially, therefore the Church decreed that once a year when the time for taking the Eucharist is near all believers should confess. Therefore, I say that delaying confession until this time, essentially speaking, is permitted but it can become unlawful accidentally, e.g., if a moment in which confession is required should be near, or if someone delays confession out of contempt. And likewise such a delay may be accidentally meritorious if he delays so that he may confess more prudently or more devoutly because of the holy season.

Therefore, we concede the first reasons.

To that which is objected on the contrary side it must be said that a physical disease, unless it is extinguished through the remedy of medicine, always grows worse if it is not perhaps also extinguished by natural power. However, the disease of sin is extinguished through contrition; so it is not a similar case.

Parallel passage: *Suppl.*, q. 6, a.5.

Article 3: Whether a parish priest ought to believe his subject when he says he confessed to another and give him the Eucharist?

On the third we proceed as follows: it seems that a parish priest ought not to believe his subject when he says he confessed to another and give him the Eucharist because of this.

1. For frequently some persons are made contrite by confession alone who were not contrite before. But a priest ought to lead his subject to good insofar as he is able. Therefore it seems he ought absolutely to ask his subject to confess to him.

2. Moreover, Proverbs 27:33 tells the pastor of a church, "Be diligent in knowing the appearance of your flock." But this cannot be done better than through confession. Therefore, he ought to demand from the subject that he confess to him.

But to the contrary: if he confesses to him, the subject could say what he wanted and the priest would believe him. Therefore, the priest ought also believe that he confessed.

I answer: it must be said that in the judicial tribunal a man is believed when he speaks against but not for himself. However, in the tribunal of penance a man is believed when he speaks for and against himself. Therefore, a distinction must be made because there may be an impediment hindering someone from taking the Eucharist in two ways. For if there is an impediment pertaining to the judicial tribunal, e.g., excommunication, the priest is not bound to believe his subject whom he knew to be excommunicate unless his absolution is evident to him. If, however, there is an impediment which pertains to the tribunal of penance, namely sin, he is bound to believe him and acts unjustly if he denies the Eucharist to one who says he confessed and was absolved by one who could absolve by apostolic authority or the authority of the bishop.

Therefore, to the first it must be said that that good which men attain in confession the person who says he confessed has already obtained if he speaks truly; if however he speaks falsely, in like manner he could speak falsely in confessing. Nor can anyone be compelled by any man's authority to confess a sin which was confessed to another who could absolve it because, as was already said, the confession of sins is part of a sacrament subject to divine and not human command.

To the second it must be said that a spiritual pastor ought diligently to recognize the appearance of his flock by considering its exterior life. But he cannot investigate more diligently than by way of confession, hence it is necessary for him to believe those things which are said to him by his subject.

Parallel passages: 4 *Sent.*, d. 17, q.3, a.3, sol. 5, ad 4; *Suppl.*, q. 8, a.5; CG 4, c. 72.

* * *

QUESTION 7: Then two questions were asked concerning these matters which pertain to clerics:
1. concerning the office of the Church, whether one who has prebends in two churches ought to recite both offices on the day on which diverse offices are performed in each church?
2. concerning the study of theology, whether someone is bound to give up the study of theology, even if he is suited to teaching others, in order to devote himself to the salvation of souls?

Article 1: Whether one who has prebends in two churches ought to recite both offices on the day on which diverse offices are performed in each church? [42]

---

[42] A prebend was a cathedral benefice, usually the revenue from one of the manors of the cathedral estate. It was designed to furnish a living for the holder. See *Oxford Dictionary of Christianity*, ed. F. L. Cross (London, 1974), "Prebends."

On the first we proceed as follows: it seems that someone in such a case ought to recite both offices.

1. For a burden ought to correspond to an emolument. Therefore, one who has the emolument of a prebend in two churches ought to bear the burden of each by reciting the office of each church.

2. Further, it seems just that if he has a greater emolument from one church in which perhaps a more extensive office is chanted, that he also take on a greater burden by reciting the more extensive office. Therefore, the choice is not his but either he ought to recite both or he ought to recite the office of the church in which he has the more lucrative benefice.

Custom was adduced to the contrary.

I answer: it must be said that, on the supposition that someone is lawfully prebended in two churches, namely because of a dispensation, we must consider that someone who received a prebend in any church is obligated to two things, namely to God to pay the praises due for his benefices, and to the church from which he receives an income. Those things which pertain to a church are subject to the dispensation of the church prelates. And therefore, the debt which he owes the church he ought to pay according to what was stipulated, either through himself if it is a prebend which requires residence, or through a vicar if this suffices according to the statute and custom of the church. The debt which he owes God he ought to pay through himself, but it does not matter to God by which psalms and hymns he praises him, for example, whether he says in Vespers "*Dixit Dominus*," or "*Laudate, pueri, Dominum*," except that a person ought to follow the traditions of his forebears. And because the praises he owes God he owes as one man, it suffices that he recite the office once according to the custom of one of the churches of which he is a cleric. Concerning the choice of office it seems reasonable that he should recite the office of that church in which he has the higher rank, e.g., if he is a dean in one and a simple canon in the other he ought to recite the office of the church in which he is a dean. If he is a simple canon in each church, he ought to recite the office of the church of higher dignity, although perhaps he has the more opulent prebend in the lesser church, because temporal matters are of no moment compared to spiritual matters. If indeed both churches are of equal dignity, he can choose whichever office he prefers if he is absent from both churches. However, if he is present in one of them he ought to conform himself to those with whom he is living.

And so the answer to the objections is clear.

Related passages concerning the obligation of office: Quodlibet 3, q. 13, a.2; 6, q. 5, a.2.

Article 2: Whether someone is bound to give up the study of theology, even if he is suited to teaching others, in order to devote himself to the salvation of souls?

On the second we proceed as follows: it seems that someone who can devote attention to the salvation of souls sins if he occupies his time in study.

1. For it is said in Galatians 6:10, "Let us do good while we have time." Also, no loss is more serious than that of time. Therefore, no one ought to spend his whole time in study, delaying to devote attention to the salvation of souls.

2. Moreover, the perfect are bound to do that which is better. But the religious are perfect so they ought especially to give up study to devote themselves to the salvation of souls.

3. Further, it is worse to wander off the moral path than a footpath. But a prelate is bound to call his subject back if he sees him wander off the footpath, therefore all the more is he bound to call him back from wandering off the moral path. But it is an error for a man to neglect what is better. Therefore a prelate ought to force a subject to apply his mind to the salvation of souls and neglect study.

On the contrary side, custom was brought in instead of reasoning.

I answer: it must be said that any two things can be compared with each other both absolutely and according to some particular case. For nothing prohibits that which is absolutely better from being the less preferred in some case, e.g., philosophizing is absolutely better than increasing your wealth but in time of necessity the latter is to be preferred. And any precious pearl is dearer than one piece of bread, but in a case of hunger the bread is to be preferred to the pearl, according to Lamentations 1:11, "They gave all valuable things for food in order to revive their souls."

However, we must consider that in any art the one who arranges the art and is called the architect is absolutely better than any manual laborer who carries out what is arranged for him by another. So also in constructing buildings, the one who arranges the building although he does no work with his hands is contracted for greater pay than the manual workers who hew the wood and cut the stones. But in a spiritual building there are the manual workers, as it were, who particularly pursue the direction of souls, e.g., by administering the sacraments or by doing some such thing in particular. But the bishops are like the principal artificers who command and arrange in what way the aforesaid workers ought to follow their office, because of which they are called "*episcopi*," i.e., superintendents. And likewise teachers of theology are like principal artificers who inquire and teach how others ought to procure the salvation of souls.

Therefore, it is absolutely better to teach theology and more meritorious if it is done with good intention, than to devote particular care to the salvation of this one and that. Whence the Apostle says concerning himself in 1 Cor. 1:17, "For Christ did not send me to baptize but to teach the Gospel," although baptizing is especially a work bearing on the salvation of souls. And in 2 Timothy 2:2, the same Apostle says, "Commit to faithful men who shall be qualified also to teach others." Reason itself also demonstrates that it is better to teach those matters pertaining to salvation to them who can be of profit both to themselves and to others than the simple people who can be of use to themselves only. However, in a particular case where necessity requires, both bishops and teachers, having interrupted their own duties, ought to devote themselves particularly to the salvation of souls.

Therefore, to the first if must be said that someone who does what is better suffers no loss of time by teaching theology, nor does someone who disposes himself to this through study.

To the second it must be said that a person is called perfect because he has perfection or because he has a state of perfection. Now human perfection consists in the charity which joins a man to God, hence Genesis 17:1 says concerning love of God, "Walk before me and be perfect." Indeed the Lord says afterwards concerning love of neighbor, "Love your enemies," and in Matthew 5:48 he concludes, "Be therefore perfect." They are said to have a state of perfection, however, who are solemnly obligated to something connected with perfection.

Now something is connected with the perfection of charity in two ways. Something is connected in one way as a preamble and something preparatory to perfection, like poverty, chastity and such by which a man is drawn back from the care of worldly things so that he has more free time for these things which are God's, whence such men are more completely instruments of perfection. Because of this Jerome, expounding the words of Peter who said in Matthew 19:27, "Behold we gave up all and followed you," says that it is not sufficient for Peter to say "Behold we gave up all," but he added what was perfect, "and followed you." [43] Therefore, those who preserve either voluntary poverty or chastity have indeed something preparatory to perfection but they are not said to have a state of perfection unless they obligate themselves to such a position by a solemn profession. Something solemn and perpetual is said to have a state, as is clear in the states of liberty, matrimony, and the like.

Something is connected to the perfection of charity in the other way as an effect, as when someone undertakes the direction of souls, for it pertains to perfect charity that someone out of love of God neglect the delight of the contemplative life which he loves more than the active and accept the occupations of the active life to procure the salvation of his neighbors. Therefore, he who applies himself in this way for the salvation of his neighbors has indeed an effect of perfection but not the state of perfection, except a bishop who, with a kind of solemn consecration, undertakes the direction of souls. Archdeacons and parish priests rather have certain duties committed to them than that they have been placed through them in a state of perfection. Therefore, only religious and bishops are said to be perfect as having the state of perfection, hence religious are made bishops but they are not made archdeacons or parish priests.

So when it is said that perfect persons are obliged to do what is better, it is true if it be understood of those who are called perfect because of the perfection of charity, for such are obligated from an inner law which binds by inclining so that they are obligated to fulfilling it according to the measure of their perfection. However, if it be understood of those who are called perfect because of a state, such as bishops and religious, it is not true for bishops are only bound to those things to which the charge of the governance undertaken extends, and religious are only bound to that to which they are

---

[43] Jerome, *Commentariorum in Mathaeum* 3, c. 19, ed. D. Hurst and M. Adriaen, CC 77: 172, lines 915-916 (Turnholti, 1969); PL 26: 143, no. 150.

obligated from the vow of their profession. Otherwise obligation would go on to infinity, but nature, art, and every law must have certain boundaries. Even given that the perfect are always bound to do that which is better, it would not be to the purpose as appears fom what was said above.

To the third it must be said that although a prelate may be bound to call his subject back from all evil, he is not bound to lead him to everything better. This reasoning too has no place in the argument as neither do the others, etc.

Parallel passages: Quodlibet 3, q. 6, a.3, ad 5; st 2-2, q. 182, a.2; 3 *Sent.*, d. 30, q.1, a.4, ad 2; d. 35, q.1, a.4, qc 2.

* * *

QUESTION 8: Then two questions were asked concerning those matters which pertain to religious:
1. whether a religious is bound to obey his prelate so as to reveal to him a secret which was committed to his trust?
2. whether he is bound to obey him so as to reveal a hidden fault of a brother which he knows?

Article 1: Whether a religious is bound to obey his prelate so as to reveal to him a secret which was committed to his trust?

Concerning the first we proceed as follows: it seems that a religious is bound to reveal to a prelate commanding it any secret committed to his trust. For by a solemn profession a religious bound himself to obey the prelate but he bound himself by a simple promise to keep the secret. Therefore, he ought to obey the prelate rather than keep the secret.

But to the contrary: Bernard says that what was instituted for the sake of charity does not militate against charity.[44] But the profession of obedience which a religious makes to a prelate was instituted for the sake of charity, therefore it does not militate against the charity by which anyone is bound to keep a neighbor's trust.

---

[44] Bernard of Clairvaux, *Tractatus de praecepto et dispensatione*, c. 2, no. 5, ed. J. Leclercq and H. Rochais, *Opera* 3: 257 (Rome, 1957 –); PL 182: 863-864.

I answer: it must be said that, as Bernard says in *De dispensatione et praecepto*, it is sufficient obedience for a religious to obey his prelate concerning those matters which pertain to the rule either directly, such as those that are written in the rule, or indirectly, such as those which can be reduced to the former as are services produced for brothers and punishments inflicted for faults and the like.[45] Now it is perfect obedience for him to obey simply in all matters which are not against the rule or against God, but it is a rash and impermissible obedience for someone to obey the prelate in these matters which are against God or against the rule.

We must therefore consider in the case under question whether it is permissible for a religious to reveal a secret committed to his trust. A distinction must be made with regard to secrets. There is a kind of secret which it is not permissible to conceal, e.g., one that tends to the danger of others from whom one is bound to avert the danger, whence it is even contained in the oath of fidelity that servants should reveal such secrets to their masters. Therefore, a religious is bound to make such a secret known on the prelate's command even if he promised not to reveal it (unless perhaps he heard it in confession because then it must in no way be revealed). As Isidore says, "In cases of bad promises, break the faith."[46] There is, however, another kind of secret which of itself can be concealed without sin, and such a secret a religious ought in no way to announce to the prelate commanding it if it is committed to his trust, for he would sin in breaking the trust committed to him.

To the first it must therefore be said that the obligation, which comes from natural law and the promise made in baptism, to keep those matters which pertain to faith and charity, is a more solemn obligation than those which come from taking religious vows.

Parallel passages: sᴛ 2-2, q. 68, a.1, ad 3; q. 70, a.1, ad 2.

Article 2: Whether a religious is bound to obey his prelate so as to reveal a fault of a brother which he knows?

Concerning the second we proceed as follows: it seems that a subject ought to reveal the hidden fault of another brother to the prelate

---

[45] Ibid., especially cc. 5 and 6, nos. 11 and 12, *Opera* 3: 261-262; ᴘʟ. 182: 867-868.

[46] Isidore of Seville, *Synonyma* 2, ᴘʟ. 83: 858, no. 58.

commanding it. Because, as Jerome says, the fault of one ought not to be hidden to the damage of the many.[47] But it must be presumed that the prelate wants to know the fault of one for the sake of the good of the many, therefore the fault of another should be revealed to a prelate commanding it.

But to the contrary: Gregory says that even if we ought sometimes to abandon some goods for the sake of obedience, we ought in no way to perpetrate something bad for the sake of obedience.[48] But dishonoring another by revealing a hidden sin seems to be bad, therefore this should not be done for the sake of obedience.

I answer: it must be said that a religious prelate presides over a chapter as an ecclesiastical judge over a judicial tribunal, whence he can obligate his subjects to make disclosure to him on command with regard to matters on which an ecclesiastical judge in a judicial tribunal can require an oath. Therefore, we must know that the way of proceeding in criminal cases is triple, one through denunciation, another through inquisition, another through accusation.

In the method of denunciation the correction of a delinquent is intended and therefore brotherly correction ought to precede this, according to the Lord in Matthew 18, so that you accuse him between yourself and him alone, but if he does not listen you should accuse him in the presence of two or three others, and lastly the matter may be related to the Church. For it pertains to charity that someone spare a brother as much as he can. Hence he ought first to strive to correct the brother's conscience, preserving his reputation by admonishing him in solitary fashion and afterwards in the presence of two or three. Finally, public repute must be disregarded in order that conscience be corrected and the affair must be related to the Church, in which process consideration is taken for conscience. For a sinner, if from the beginning he saw his sin made public, would lose shame and be made to sin more obstinately.

Indeed ill report ought to come first in inquisition, and in accusation a written statement through which the accuser obligates himself to recompense ought to come first. However, in inquisition

---

[47] I have been unable to find this passage in Jerome.
[48] Gregory the Great, *Moralia* 35, c. 14, ed. M. Adriaen (Turnholti, 1979); PL 76: 766, no. 19.

and accusation the punishment of the sinner is intended for the good of the many. Therefore, if the accuser who obligates himself to recompense should appear in the chapter, the prelate can by a command demand a confession of truth as also an ecclesiastical judge can demand an oath. And likewise, if ill report comes first, the prelate can by a command ascertain the truth and the subjects are bound to obey. If, however, the process is one of simple denunciation, the religious is not bound by the prelate giving the command to reveal a brother's fault unless he sees him uncorrected by a preceding warning. Rather he would sin more if he revealed it on the prelate's command because he is bound more strongly to obey the Gospel than the prelate. And the prelate would sin much more if he were to lead his subject to pervert the order of the Gospel.

To the first it must be stated that with respect to a past sin on which one has been corrected already by a secret admonition or on which it can be hoped that one will be corrected, unless the contrary is found to be the case, there can be no threat of danger to the multitude. Still, the objection goes forward concerning a future sin which is dangerous to the multitude, either spiritually or corporeally, for then it is not necessary to wait for a secret admonition, but rather it is necessary to oppose the danger immediately. Whence also the Lord does not say, "if he intends to sin in the future," but "if he has sinned in the past" (Matthew 18:15).

Parallel passages: Quodlibet 4, q. 8, a.1; ST 2-2, q. 70, a.1; 4 *Sent.*, d. 19, q.2, a.3, qc 1, ad 5.

* * *

QUESTION 9: Then four questions pertaining to sin were asked:
1. whether sin is some sort of nature?
2. whether perjury is a more serious sin than homicide?
3. whether a person sins who out of ignorance does not observe a papal constitution?
4. whether a monk sins mortally in eating meat?

Article 1: Whether sin is some sort of nature?

On the first we proceeded as follows: it seems that sin is not some sort of nature. For John 1:3 says, "Without him nothing was made," i.e., sin. But what is a nature cannot be called nothing, therefore sin is not some sort of nature.

But to the contrary: if sin is not some sort of nature it is necessarily a pure privation. But pure privations like death and darkness do not admit of degrees of more and less. Therefore, one sin would not be more serious than another, which is incoherent.

I answer: it must be said that a sin, especially of transgression, is a disorderly act. On the part of the act, therefore, sin is some sort of nature. But lack of order is a privation and according to this sin is called nothing.[49] And through this the solution to the objections is clear.

Parallel passages: 2 *Sent.*, d. 37, q.1, a.1; *De malo*, q. 2, a.1, ad 4.

Article 2: Whether perjury is a more serious sin than homicide?

Concerning the second we proceeded as follows: it seems that perjury is a more serious sin than homicide.

1. For Bernard says that neither God nor man can dispense from the precepts of the first table, however God but not man can dispense from the precepts of the second table.[50] From this we can understand that it is more serious to sin against the precepts of the first table than against the precepts of the second. But perjury is against the precept of the first table which is "Do not take the name of your God in vain;" homicide, however, is against the precept of the second table, "Do not kill." Therefore, perjury is a more serious sin than homicide.

2. Moreover, it is more serious to sin against God than against man. But perjury is a sin against God, homicide a sin against man; therefore perjury is a more serious sin than homicide.

But to the contrary: punishment is proportioned to the fault but homicide is punished more severely than perjury so it is the more serious sin.

I answer: it must be said that, as the Apostle says in Hebrews 6:16, "Men swear by what is greater than themselves and an oath puts an

---

[49] The notion of sin as privation derives ultimately from the Neoplatonists through Augustine. See, for example, *De civitate Dei* 11, c. 22, CSEL 40: 542-544; CC 48: 340-341; PL 41: 335-336; and 12, c. 7, CSEL 40: 577; CC 48: 362; PL 41: 355; and *Enchiridion* 4, no. 12, ed. M. van den Hont, CC 46: 54 (Turnholti, 1969); PL 40: 236-237.

[50] Bernard of Clairvaux, *Tractatus de precepto*, c. 3, *Opera* 3: 257-259; PL 182: 502-503.

end to all their wrangling." However, in the case of homicide an oath would be the end of wrangling uselessly if homicide were a more serious fault than perjury, for it would be presumed that someone who committed the greater fault of homicide would not fear to incur the lesser one of perjury. So because an oath is deposed in the case of any sin, it is clearly shown that perjury ought to be held the greatest sin, nor undeservedly because to perjure the name of God seems to be a kind of denial of the divine name, so the sin of perjury holds second place after idolatry, as appears from the order of the precepts. But also with the Gentiles an oath was most honored, as is said in *Metaphysica* 1.[51]

We grant the first reasons.

To what is objected on the contrary side: it must be stated that in human judgment the quantity of punishment does not always correspond to the quantity of the fault for sometimes a greater punishment is inflicted for a lesser fault, when more serious harm threatens men from the lesser fault. But according to God's judgment, the more serious fault is punished by the more severe punishment. Whence so that the gravity of idolatry and perjury might be shown, after he said in the first precept, "You will not adore nor worship those," it is added in Exodus 20:5, "I am the Lord your God visiting the iniquities of the fathers on the sons." And after he said (verse 7), "Do not take the name of the Lord your God in vain," he adds, "for the Lord will not hold him who takes his name in vain guiltless."

Parallel passages: Quodlibet 5, q. 10, a.2; st 2-2, q. 70, a.4, ad 3.

Article 3: Whether a person sins who out of ignorance does not observe a papal constitution?

On the third we proceed as follows: it seems that he who acts against a papal constitution through ignorance, does not sin.

1. For as Augustine says, sin is voluntary to the extent that if there is no voluntary, then there is no sin.[52] But ignorance causes the involuntary, as is said in *Ethica* 3.[53] Therefore, what is done through ignorance is not a sin.

---

[51] Aristotle, *Metaphysica* 1.3, 983b35, *Works*, vol. 8.

[52] Augustine, *De libero arbitrio* 3, c. 1, ed. Wm. Green, csel. 74 (Vienna, 1956); pl. 32.

[53] Aristotle, *Ethica nicomachea* 3.50, *Works*, vol. 9.

2. Further, according to the laws a lord can reclaim his appointed servant after a certain time. This, however, ought to be computed from the time of its being known, not from the time of the decree.[54] Therefore, the obligation to a papal constitution binds from the time of its being known.

But to the contrary: ignorance of the law does not excuse anyone. But a papal constitution makes the law so he who acts against a papal constitution through ignorance is not excused.

I answer: it must be stated that the ignorance which is the cause of an act causes the involuntary, hence it always excuses unless the ignorance iself is a sin, which happens when someone does not know what he is able to know and he is obliged to know. Now indeed everyone is obliged to know the papal constitution in his fashion. If, therefore, someone does not know this through negligence, he is not excused from blame if he acts against the constitution. If indeed there was a sufficient obstacle to someone's knowing it, e.g., if he was in prison or in foreign lands which the constitution did not reach, or because of something similar, such ignorance excuses so that he does not sin by acting against the pope's constitution.

The response to the objections is clear.

Parallel passages: ST 1-2, q. 90, a.4; *De ver.*, q. 17, a.3; *De malo*, q. 3, a.7 and a.8.

Article 4: Whether a monk sins mortally in eating meat?

Concerning the fourth we proceed as follows: it seems that a monk sins mortally in eating meat.

1. For the canon law *De consecratione*, d. 5, in the chapter "*Carnem*," says that monks ought not to eat meat and if they do the contrary they ought to be incarcerated.[55] But such punishment is only inflicted for a mortal sin, therefore monks sin mortally in eating meat.

2. Moreover, it is a mortal sin to act against a vow. But monks are obligated from a vow to keep blessed Benedict's Rule in which it is

---

[54] Reading "a tempore notitiae, non a tempore ordinationis" istead of "a tempore ordinationis, non a tempore notitiae," according to the suggestion in the Vives edition, p. 374, note 3.

[55] Gratian, *Decretum* 3, d. 5, c. 32, ed. A. R. Richter, *Corpus juris canonici* 1: 1237 (Leipzig, 1839); PL 187: 1865.

said that monks should abstain from meat. Therefore, monks sin mortally in eating meat.

But to the contrary: no mortal sin is allowed anyone by reason of an infirmity, but eating meat is allowed a monk by reason of infirmity. Therefore, it is not a mortal sin for a monk to eat meat.

I answer: it must be stated that essentially speaking, nothing is a mortal sin for any monk or religious which is not a mortal sin for another person except it be contrary to what the very vow of the profession obligated him; accidentally speaking, however, because it provides an occasion for sin, something can be a sin for him which would not be a sin for another person. Therefore we must consider what it is to which a religious is bound by the vow of profession.

If indeed a religious in making profession vowed he was going to observe the Rule, he would seem to obligate himself by the vow to the individual matters which are contained in the Rule and so, in acting against any of them, he would sin mortally. From this it would follow that the state of religious life would be a snare of mortal sin to the religious which he would scarcely or never be able to avoid. Therefore, the holy fathers who instituted the orders, not wanting men to embrace the snare of damnation but rather the way of salvation, arranged such a form of profession in which that danger could not exist, as in the Order of Friars Preachers there is the most careful and secure form of avowal which does not involve a promise to observe the Rule but "obedience according to the Rule." Hence from the vow they are obligated to observe those matters which are put in the Rule as precepts and which the prelate according to the tenor of the Rule wanted to command. Other matters which are not contained in the Rule under a precept do not fall directly under the vow so that one does not sin mortally in omitting those.

The blessed Benedict indeed did not decree that a monk should promise to observe the Rule, but he decreed that the one professing promise the conversion of his morals according to the Rule. This is what is expressed: that he direct his morals according to the Rule, which he acts against if he transgresses either the precepts in the Rule or even holds the Rule in contempt by refusing to direct his acts entirely according to it. But not all points contained in the Rule are precepts, for some are warnings or counsels; some however are orders or statutes such as that no one may speak after Compline. Such statutes, however, which are contained in the Rule do not have the power of precepts. Neither does a prelate in decreeing something always intend to bind someone under pain of mortal sin through the precept. Now the prelate is a sort of living rule. So it would be foolish to hold that a monk breaking silence after Compline sins mortally, unless perhaps he does this against a precept of the prelate or from contempt of the Rule. Abstention from meat, however, is not included in blessed Benedict's Rule as a precept but as a sort of statute, hence a monk in eating meat does not from this very act sin mortally, except in the case of disobedience or contempt.

Therefore, to the first it must be stated that punishment is inflicted on a monk for obstinately and disobediently eating meat.

To the second it must be stated that eating meat is not against a monk's vow except when he eats it out of disobedience or contempt.

What is objected on the contrary side has no efficacy for it holds good concerning these things which are bad in themselves, such as homicide, adultery and the like, which are illicit for all, the healthy as well as the infirm. It does not, however, hold good concerning these things which are bad because they are prohibited, for something can be prohibited for the healthy which is not prohibited for the sick.

Parallel passage: ST 2-2, q. 186, a.9.

* * *

QUESTION 10: Then with regard to the good in the order of glory two questions were asked about glorified bodies:
1. whether a glorified body can exist naturally in the same place with another nonglorified body?
2. whether this can be accomplished miraculously?

Article 1: Whether a glorified body can exist naturally in the same place with another nonglorified body?

On the first we proceed as follows: it seems that a glorified body can naturally exist in the same place with another body.

1. For if it is prohibited from existing in the same place with another, it is either because of density or fleshiness, or because of dimensions. But it is not because of density or fleshiness because a glorified body will be spiritual according to the Apostle (1 Cor. 15:44); likewise it is not because of dimensions either, for since things that

touch each other are those whose ends are together, it is necessary for a point of one natural body to be together with a point of another, and a line with a line, and a surface with a surface. Therefore for the same reason a body with a body also. Therefore, a glorified body is not prohibited from being able to exist naturally with another body in the same place.

2. Moreover, the Commentator says on *Physica* 8 that the parts of air and water partly penetrate each other because they are partly of a spiritual nature.[56] But glorified bodies will be entirely spiritual as we already said, therefore they will be able to penetrate other bodies totally and likewise exist with them.

But to the contrary: glorification does not remove a nature. But a human body cannot naturally exist together with another body in the same place in this state, therefore neither can it after it is glorified.

I answer: it must be stated that it is clear that a human body in this state cannot exist in the same place with another body. If, therefore, a glorified body can naturally exist with another body in the same place because of some property engrafted on it, that property removes this which prohibits the human body's existing in the same place with another body in this state. We must, therefore, consider what such a prohibiting factor may be.

Some say that this property is a density or fleshiness which is removed through the dowry of glory which they name subtlety.[57] But this is not intelligible for we cannot ascertain what such fleshiness or density is. It is not a quality because there is no quality which when it is removed the body to which it belongs can exist with another body in the same place. Likewise it cannot be the form or matter which are parts of the essence, because then the whole essence of the human body would not remain in glory, which is a heretical opinion. Therefore, we must say that the prohibiting factor is nothing but the dimensions which corporeal matter sustains. For it is necessary that that which is of itself be the cause in any genus; however, distinction according to position first and of itself belongs to dimensional

---

[56] Averroes, *Physica* 8, *Opera* 4: 430v.

[57] See Albert the Great, *Sententiae* 4, d. 44, a.23, *Opera* 28, and Bonaventure, *Sententiae* 4, p. 2, sect. 2, a.3, q.1, Quaracchi ed., 4. Also see Augustine, *De civitate Dei* 13, c. 22 and c. 23, CSEL 40: 646-652; CC 48: 405-408; PL 41: 395-398.

quantity which is defined as quantity having position, and that whence the parts in a subject, from this [fact] that they are subject to dimension, have a distinction according to position. And just as there is a distinction of diverse parts of one body according to the diverse parts of one place through dimensions, so because of dimensions diverse bodies are distinguished according to diverse places. For actual division makes two bodies of physical matter, however potential divisibility makes two parts of one body, hence the Philosopher says in *Physica* 4 that just as when a wooden cube is inserted into water or air it necessarily displaces only water or air, so it would be necessary that if we posited a void, the separated dimensions would displace it.[58] Therefore, since glory does not remove a body's dimensions, I say that a glorified body cannot naturally exist with another body in the same place because of any engrafted property.

Therefore, to the first it must be stated that as was said, a human body in that state is prohibited from existing with another body in the same place not because of a fleshiness or density which is removed through glory (for the Apostle opposes spirituality to the animality according to which a body needs nourishment, as Augustine says; however, he does not oppose it to fleshiness or density) but it is impeded because of the dimensions.[59] Indeed the reason which is given on the contrary side is placed among the sophistical reasons by the Philosopher in *Physica* 6, for place is not owing to a point, a line, and a surface, but to a body.[60] So it does not follow that if the boundaries of bodies are touching each other at the same time that because of this fact many bodies can exist in the same place.

To the second it must be stated as the Commentator says in the same place, that penetration is made through condensation and they are said to have spiritual power because of rarity. However, it would be erroneous to say that glorified bodies are spiritual in this way because they are similar to air and wind, as is clear through what Gregory says in *Moralium* 14.[61]

Parallel passages: the next article; *Suppl.*, q. 83, a.4.

---

[58]   Aristotle, *Physica* 4.8, 216a26 ff., *Works*, vol. 2.

[59]   Augustine, see note 57 above.

[60]   Aristotle, *Physica* 4.1, 209a8-13, *Works*, vol. 2.

[61]   Gregory the Great, *Moralia* 14, c. 55, cc 143A: 743, no. 71; pl 75: 1077.

Article 2: Whether this can be accomplished miraculously?

On the second we proceed as follows: it seems that a glorified body can in no way exist with another body in the same place at the same time.

1. For just as one body is related to one place, so are two bodies to two places. Therefore, with substitutions, just as one body is related to two places so are two bodies to one place. But one body can in no way exist in two places, therefore neither can two bodies exist in one place.

2. Moreover, if two bodies exist in one place then two points are assumed in the two extremities of the place. It follows, therefore, that between these two points there will be two straight lines of the two bodies existing in the same place, which is impossible. Therefore, it is impossible for two bodies to exist in the same place.

But to the contrary: it is said in John 20 that Christ entered where his disciples were though the doors were closed, which cannot be unless his body existed in the same place simultaneously with the corporeal doors. A glorified body can, therefore, exist with another body in the same place.

I answer: it must be stated that, as we already said, two bodies are prohibited by their dimensions from existing in the same place because corporeal matter is divided according to dimensions; however dimensions are distinguished according to position. But God, who is the first cause of everything, can conserve an effect in existence without its proximate causes. Hence, just as he conserves accidents without a subject in the sacrament of the altar, so can he conserve distinction of corporeal matter and the dimensions in it without diversity of place. Therefore, it can be miraculously accomplished that two bodies exist in the same place. So the saints attributed to Christ's body that it existed through the closed womb of the Virgin and entered through closed doors by means of divine power. And I say likewise that a glorified body which will be fashioned in conformity with Christ's radiant body will be able to exist with another body in the same place, not because of some engrafted created power but only with the aid and action of the divine power, just as the body of Peter cured the sick by its shadow, but was performing miracles with the aid of divine power.

Therefore, to the first it must be stated that we must employ it thus with the proportion changed: as the first is related to the second as two to three, so is the third related to the fourth. Therefore, with substitutions, as the first is related to the third so also is the second to the fourth, i.e., three to six. And the reasoning should proceed according to this thus: as one body is related to one place so are two bodies to two places, and therefore as one body to two bodies, so one place to two places. And so it does not follow that if one body cannot exist in two places that two bodies cannot exist in one place. One body's existing in two places implies a contradiction because it pertains to the intelligible structure of place to be the boundary of the thing in place. However, a boundary is that outside of which nothing belongs to the thing, hence nothing of the thing in a place can exist in an exterior place. Because if it is maintained that it exists in two places, it follows that it is outside its own place and so it follows that it is in a place and not in a place. Nor is there a valid disclaimer concerning Christ's body because it is not in the sacrament of the altar by way of place but rather through conversion.

To the second it must be stated that for two straight mathematical lines to be between two points is impossible because we can understand no reason for their distinction except position. But for two natural lines to be between two points is indeed naturally impossible but possible through a miracle because there is another reason for the distinction of the two lines from the diversity of the underlying bodies which are conserved by divine power even when diversity of position is removed.

Parallel passages: sт 3, q. 54, a.1, ad 1; q. 57, a.4, ad 2; *Suppl.*, q. 83, aa.3-4; cG 4, c. 87; *In Ioann.*, c. 20, lect. 4; 1 *ad Cor.*, c. 15, lect. 6.

Second Quodlibet

Questions were asked concerning Christ, angels, and men.

QUESTION 1: Concerning Christ, two questions were asked about his passion:
1. whether he was numerically the same man during the three days of death?
2. whether any suffering of Christ would have sufficed for the redemption of mankind without death?

Article 1: Whether Christ was the same man during the three days of death?

On the first we proceed as follows: it seems that Christ was the same man during the three days.

1. For Matthew 12:40 says, "As Jonah was in the belly of the whale for three days and three nights, so will the son of man be in the heart of the earth." But the son of man in the heart of the earth was not other than the son of man who spoke on earth, otherwise Christ would have been two sons. Therefore, he was the same man during the three days of death.

2. Further, Jonah was the same man in the whale's belly as he was before. But as Jonah was in the whale's belly so was Christ in the heart of the earth. Therefore Christ was also the same man.

But to the contrary: if the form of the part is removed, the form of the whole which results from the composition of form and matter is removed. Now during the three days of death Christ's soul was separated from his body, therefore his humanity ceased to exist. So he was not numerically the same man during the three days of death.

I answer: it must be said that three substances were united in Christ – body, soul, and divinity. Now body and soul were not only united in one person but in one nature, but divinity could not be united in a nature either to soul or body because, since it is the most perfect nature, it cannot be a part of any nature. Yet it was united to body and soul in the person. In death, however, Christ's soul was separated from his body, otherwise his death would not have been a true death, for by definition death is the separation of the soul from the body on which it bestows life. But divinity was not separated from either the body or the soul, which is clear from the Creed which says of the Son of God that "He was buried and descended into hell." However, the body lying in the tomb and the soul descending into hell would not be attributed to the Son of God unless these two were joined to him in a unity of person or hypostasis.[1]

And therefore, we can speak of Christ during the three days of death in two ways: with regard to the hypostasis or person, and in this way he is during the three days absolutely numerically the same as he was; or with regard to the human nature, and this in two ways. If we speak with regard to the whole nature which is called humanity, Christ was not a man during the three days of death and so neither the same nor another man, but rather the same hypostasis. If we speak with regard to a part of the human nature, his soul was indeed entirely the same numerically because it was not transformed in substance; the body was numerically the same according to matter but not according to the substantial form which is the soul. So we cannot say that he was absolutely numerically the same because any substantial difference excludes absolute sameness. However, *animate* is a substantial difference and therefore to die is to be corrupted and not only to be altered. Nor on the other hand can we say that he was absolutely nonidentical or other because he was not nonidentical or other according to his whole substance.[2] We must therefore say that he was the same in one respect and not the same in another respect, for he was the same with respect to matter but not the same with respect to form.

Therefore, to the first it must be said that 'man' denotes a nature, but 'son' denotes a hypostasis and so Christ can be called 'son of man' rather than 'man' during the three days of death.

---

[1] On person and hypostasis see note 12 to Quodlibet 1 above.

[2] The Latin word for 'other' here is *aliud* which signifies otherness or diversity of substance (as nature or supposit). *Aliud simpliciter* means otherness according to supposit, not nature; otherness according to nature is signified by *aliud secundum quid*. See sт 3, q. 17, a.1, ad 7, Blackfriars ed., 50: 56.

To the second it must be said that that passage does not mean likeness with regard to everything but only with regard to occupation [of a place], for Christ was dead in the heart of the earth but Jonah was not dead in the whale's belly.

Parallel passages: 3 *Sent.*, d. 22, q.1, a.1; Quodlibet 4, q. 5; sᴛ 3, q. 50, a.4; *Comp. theol.*, c. 229.

Article 2: Whether any other suffering of Christ would have sufficed for the redemption of mankind without his death?

On the second we proceed as follows: it seems that no other suffering of Christ would have sufficed for the redemption of mankind without his death.

1. For the Apostle says in Galatians 2:21, "If there is justice from the law then Christ died in vain," that is uselessly and without cause. But if any other suffering sufficed then Christ died in vain. Now the Apostle regards this as inadmissible. Therefore, no other suffering of Christ would have sufficed for the redemption of mankind.

2. Moreover, that is said to be bought which is procured for a just price.[3] Now a just price for the sin of the first parent by which mankind was sold into bondage could not be other than the life of Christ which is worth the lives of all men, which lives are removed through that sin, for through the first man's sin death entered into all, as Romans 5 says. Therefore, mankind could not have been redeemed through any other suffering of Christ without his death.

3. Further, Gregory says in *Moralium* 3 that "unless Christ had taken on himself an undeserved death, by no means would he free us from a deserved death."[4] Therefore, no other suffering would have sufficed for mankind's liberation without his death.

4. Further, the Apostle says in Hebrews 10:14, that Christ "by one offering perfected forever those who are sanctified," and therefore there is no place for a second offering. But it is clear that Christ sustained many kinds of suffering before death – hungering, laboring, being spat upon, being beaten. If, therefore, these sufferings had sufficed he would not have offered himself for death. Yet he offered himself as a sacrifice to God for our sins, as is said in Ephesians 5, and

---

[3] On just price, see below, q. 5, a.2.

[4] Gregory the Great, *Moralia* 3, c. 14, ᴄᴄ 143: 132, no. 27, lines 40 and 41; ᴘʟ 75: 613, no. 27.

this he did through his death. Therefore the suffering of Christ without his death would not have sufficed.

But to the contrary: anyone's injury or suffering is measured from the dignity of his person, for a king suffers a greater injury if he is struck in the face than does any private person. But the dignity of Christ's person is infinite because he is a divine person; so any suffering of his, however little it be, is infinite. Therefore, any suffering of his would have sufficed for the redemption of mankind even without his death. Moreover, Bernard says that the least drop of Christ's blood would have sufficed for the redemption of mankind.[5] However, a drop of Christ's blood could have been shed without his death, so even without his death he could have redeemed mankind through any suffering.

I answer: it must be said that two things are required for buying, namely the amount of the price and its allotment for buying something. For if someone should give a price not equivalent for acquiring something, there is not said to be a purchase absolutely but partly a purchase and partly a gift. For example, if someone should buy a book which is worth twenty libras for ten, he would partly buy the book and it would partly be given to him. On the other hand, if he should give an even greater price and not allot it for buying he would not be said to buy the book. Therefore, if we speak of mankind's redemption with regard to the amount of the price, so any suffering of Christ, even without his death, would have sufficed for the redemption of mankind because of the infinite dignity of the person. And in this manner the last two reasons proceed. If, however, we speak with regard to the allotment of the price, we must say that Christ's other sufferings without his death are not allotted for the redemption of mankind by God the Father and Christ. And there are three reasons for this. First, in order that the price of mankind's redemption might not only be infinite in value but also of the same genus, i.e., in order that he might redeem us from death through death. Second, in order that Christ's death might not only be the price of the redemption but also an example of virtue, namely in order that men should not fear to die for the truth. And the Apostle assigns these two causes in Hebrews 2:14-15 saying, "In order that through death

---

[5] I have not been able to locate this passage in the works of Bernard of Clairvaux.

he might destroy him who had command of death," as concerns the first, "and might free them who through their whole lives were subject to servitude through the fear of death," as regards the second. Third, in order that his death might also be a sacrament of salvation while we die to sin and carnal desires and our own feelings by the power of Christ's death. And this cause is assigned in 1 Peter 3:18: "Christ died once for our sins, the just for the unjust, in order that he might offer us to God, dead indeed in the flesh but brought to life in the spirit." And therefore, mankind is not redeemed through any other suffering without the death of Christ.

Therefore, to the first it must be said that Christ's death is not allotted for the redemption of mankind without cause, although a lesser suffering could have sufficed as we said.

To the second it must be said that Christ would have paid a sufficient price for mankind's redemption not by paying with his life but even by undergoing any suffering if a lesser one had been divinely allotted for this. And this is because of the infinite dignity of the person of Christ, as we said.

The other two reasons proceed from the fact that Christ's other sufferings were not allotted so that mankind would be redeemed through them without Christ's death.

Parallel passages: st 3, q. 46, a.2; q. 50, a.1; q. 52, a.1; cg 4, c. 55; *Comp. theol.*, c. 227; *Contra errores Graecorum* etc., c. 7; 3 *Sent.*, d. 20, a.3.

* * *

Then questions were asked about angels: first as to their composition, second as to the time of their motion.

QUESTION 2: Concerning the composition of angels two questions were asked:
   1. whether an angel is a composite of essence and being (*esse*) in the manner of a substance?
   2. whether supposit and nature are diverse in an angel?

Article 1: Whether an angel is composed of essence and being (*esse*) in the manner of a substance?

On the first we proceed as follows: it seems that an angel is not composed of essence and being in the manner of a substance.

1. For the essence of an angel is the angel itself, because the quiddity of a simple thing is the simple thing itself. If, therefore, an angel were composed of being and essence, it would be composed of itself and another. But this is incoherent. So it is not composed of being and essence in the manner of a substance.

2. Moreover, no accident enters into the substantial composition of a substance. But an angel's being is an accident, for Hilary attributes properly to God in *De trinitate* that being is not an accident in him but is subsisting truth.[6] Therefore, an angel is not composed of essence and being in the manner of an essence.

But to the contrary: the commentary on *De causis* says that "An intelligence, which we call an angel, has essence and being." [7]

I answer: it must be said that something is predicated of something in two ways – in the manner of an essence or in the manner of participation. 'Light' is predicated of an illumined body in the manner of participation, but if there were some separated light then it would be predicated of it in the manner of an essence. Therefore, we must say that 'being' (*ens*) is predicated in the manner of an essence of God alone, inasmuch as divine being (*esse*) is subsistent and absolute being. However, it is predicated of any creature in the manner of participation, for no creature is its being but rather is something which has being.[8] So also we call God 'good' in the manner of an essence because he is goodness itself, we call creatures 'good' in the manner of participation because they have goodness. For anything is good inasmuch as it is, according to what Augustine says in *De doctrina christiana* 1, that inasmuch as we are we are good.[9] However, whenever something is predicated of another in the manner of participation, it is necessary that there be something in the latter besides that in which it participates. And therefore, in any creature the creature itself which has being and its very being are

---

[6] Hilary of Poitiers, *De trinitate* 7, ed. P. Smulders, cc 62, part 1 (Turnholti, 1980); PL 10: 234, no 41.

[7] Averroes, *De causis*, Prop. 7, *Opera*, vol. 7.

[8] See pp. 18-21 above and accompanying footnotes.

[9] Augustine, *De doctrina christiana* 1, c. 32, ed. J. Martin, cc 32: 26, line 4 (Turnholti, 1962); PL 34: 32.

other, and this is what Boethius says in *De hebdomabidus*, that being and what is are diverse in all entities except the first.[10]

But it must be known that something is participated in in two ways. In one way it is participated in as though belonging to the substance of the thing participating, as a genus is participated in by a species of it. However, a creature does not participate in being this way for that belongs to the substance of a thing which enters into its definition, but being (*ens*) is not included in the definition of a creature because it is neither a genus nor a difference. So it is participated in as something not belonging to the thing's essence.[11] And therefore, the question 'Is it?' is different from the question 'What is it?' So, since all that is outside a thing's essence may be called an accident, the being which pertains to the question 'Is it?' is an accident. Therefore, the Commentator says on *Metaphysica* 5 that this proposition, 'Socrates is,' is an accidental predication when it signifies either a thing's being (*entitatem*) or the truth of a proposition.[12]

But it is true that this noun 'being' (*ens*), when it signifies a thing to which such being (*esse*) is attributable, signifies the thing's essence and according to this signification being is divided into the ten categories. But it does not signify univocally because it is not attributable to all things by the same intelligible notion but is attributable to substance through itself (*per se*) and to the other categories in another fashion.[13] Therefore, if there is composition in

---

[10] Boethius, *Quomodo substantiae in eo quod sint, bonae sint*, ed. E. K. Rand, *The Theological Tractates* (Cambridge, Mass., 1918; rept. 1962), pp. 38-50; PL 64: 1311-1312. Boethius here distinguishes *id quod est* or the thing which exists (the substance), and the *esse* or that by which the substance exists. These are distinct in composite things but not in simple in simple beings.

[11] See pp. 18-21 and accompanying footnotes.

[12] Averroes, *Metaphysica* 5, c. 7, *Opera*, 8: 116v-117r.

[13] Some terms, according to St. Thomas, are predicated of several things univocally when they have exactly the same intelligible notion or meaning in each such predication. Others are predicated equivocally, i.e., the same term has different meanings in the several predications as does 'rare' in 'This coin is rare' and 'This steak is rare.' Still others are predicated analogously, i.e., with a meaning that is partly the same and partly different. Here the predications express different relationships but are referred to one and the same thing. 'Being', for example, is predicated of different things in relation to one thing, a subject. Thus substances are said to be beings because they have being of themselves while accidents are said to be beings because they inhere in substances as their subjects. Hence as St. Thomas says, 'being' is predicated of 'substance' in one way and of the other categories in another way. See also *De principiis*

an angel of essence and being, this is not a composition as from the parts of a substance but as from a substance and what adheres to the substance.

Therefore, to the first it must be said that sometimes a third thing results from those which are joined together; as the humanity by which a man is a man is constituted from soul and body so a man is composed of soul and body.[14] Sometimes, however, a third thing does not result from those which are joined together but a kind of composite intelligible notion results, as when the notions 'man' and 'white' go to make up the intelligible notion 'white man'. And in such things something is composed of itself and another, just as a white thing is composed of that which is white and whiteness.

To the second it must be said that being is an accident, not as though related accidentally to a substance, but as the actuality of any substance. Hence God himself, who is his own actuality, is his own being.[15]

Parallel passages: st 1, q. 50, a.2, ad 3; q. 75, a.5, ad 4; 1 *Sent.*, d. 8, q.5, a.1; 2, d. 3, q.1, a.1; cg 2, c. 52; *De pot.*, q. 7, a.4.

Article 2: Whether supposit and nature are the same in an angel?

On the second we proceed as follows: it seems that supposit and nature are the same in an angel.

---

naturae 6, Leonine ed., 43; *In metaphysica* 4, nos. 535-539, and 7, no. 1334, Marietti ed. On the doctrine of analogy in general, see Geo. P. Klubertanz, *St. Thomas Aquinas on Analogy* (Chicago, 1960); Ralph McInerny, *The Logic of Analogy* (The Hague, 1961); Eric L. Mascall, *Existence and Analogy* (London, 1949); Jos. Owens, "Analogy as a Thomistic Approach to Being," *Mediaeval Studies* 24 (1962), 303-322; Geo. Phelan, *St. Thomas and Analogy* (Milwaukee, 1941); James Ross, "A New Theory of Analogy," *Proceedings of the American Catholic Philosophical Association* 44 (1970), 70-85.

[14] The Latin text in both the Vives and Marietti editions reads: "aliquando ex his quae simul iunguntur, relinquitur aliqua res tertia, sicuti ex anima et corpore constituitur humanitas, quae est homo...." Yet for St. Thomas, humanity is not the man but that by which (*qua*) a man is a man (see pp. 21-23 above). A man has humanity but is not humanity. I have thus translated *qua* here rather than *quae* to avoid misunderstanding.

[15] Being is not an accident but is spoken of as an accident on the grounds that it, like accidents, is external to the essence of a thing. See also *De ente et essentia* 6, ed. Boyer, pp. 49-51 and *De potentia*, q. 5, a.4, ad 3, Marietti ed., p. 139b.

1. For in these things which are composed of matter and form, supposit and nature differ because the supposit adds individual matter to the nature of the species. This cannot be the case in an angel if the angel is not composed of matter and form. Therefore, supposit and nature do not differ in an angel.

2. But it was objected that in an angel the supposit differs from the nature inasmuch as the supposit is understood as something which has being but the nature is not. But to the contrary: just as being is not put in the definition of a nature so it would not be put in the definition of a supposit or singular if the supposit or singular were defined. Therefore, the supposit does not differ from the nature through being so supposit and nature differ in no way.

But to the contrary: in all creatures a nature constitutes a supposit. But nothing constitutes itself, so in no creature are supposit and nature the same.

I answer: it must be stated that in order to understand this question, it is necessary to consider what supposit and nature are.[16] Although we speak of nature in many ways, in one way we call the very substance of a thing the nature, insofar as 'substance' signifies a thing's essence or quiddity or what a thing is, as is said in *Metaphysica* 5.[17] Therefore, as we use the term here 'nature' signifies what a definition signifies. Thus Boethius in *De duabus naturis* says that "nature is anything which a specific difference gives form to," for the specific difference completes the definition.[18] But a supposit is a singular in the category of substance, and is called a hypostasis or first substance. And because sensible substances composed of matter and form are better known to us, let us first see how essence or nature is related to supposit in them.

Some say that the form of the part is really the same as the form of the whole which is called the essence or nature and differs from it only conceptually.[19] For it is called the form of the part inasmuch as it

---

[16] See also sт 1, q. 3, a.3, Blackfriars ed., 2: 28-31 and 3, q. 2, a.2, Blackfriars ed., 48: 42-43.

[17] Aristotle, *Metaphysica* 5.4, 1014b35-1015a13, *Works*, vol. 8.

[18] Boethius, *Liber contra Eutychen*, c. 1, ed. E. K. Rand, *The Theological Tractates* (Cambridge, Mass., 1918; rept. 1962); pl 64: 1342в.

[19] According to St. Thomas, *In metaphysica* 7, lect. 9, nos. 1467-1469, Marietti ed., this was the opinion of Averroes and some of his followers. See Averroes, *Metaphysica* 5.5 and 7.4, *Opera*, 8: 86r, 90r, 93v.

makes matter actually exist, but the form of the whole inasmuch as it constitutes the species.[20] Thus the soul is called the form of the part inasmuch as it makes the body actually exist, and likewise the form of the whole inasmuch as it constitutes the human species (and in this way it is called humanity). And according to this position, in things composed of matter and form the nature is part of the supposit for the supposit is an individual composed of matter and form, as we said.

But the aforementioned position does not seem to be true because the nature or essence is that which a definition signifies. Yet a definition in natural things signifies not only form but also matter, as is said in *Metaphysica* 6.[21] Nor can it be said that matter is put in the definition of a natural thing as something not belonging to its essence, for it is proper to an accident to be defined through something which is not its essence, namely through its subject, and therefore it has essence incompletely as *Metaphysica* 6 says.[22] The only remaining possibility, therefore, is that in things composed of matter and form the essence or nature is not the form alone but the composite of matter and form.

It remains to be considered whether, since a supposit or natural individual is composed of matter and form, it is the same as its essence or nature. And the Philosopher raises the question in *Metaphysica* 7 where he inquires whether a thing and its quiddity are the same.[23] And he determines that in cases of *per se* predication they are the same, but where there is predication *per accidens*, they are not the same.[24] For a man is nothing other than that which is essential to man, for 'man' signifies nothing but a biped animal capable of walking. But a white thing is not entirely the same as the essence white which is signified by the term 'white' for 'white' only signifies a quality, as is said in the *Categoriae*; however a white thing is a

[20] The form of the part is the substantial form, e.g., the rational soul in a man. The form of the whole is the essence or quiddity which embraces both form and matter as essential principles but which prescinds from designated matter. For a man, the form of the whole is humanity.

[21] Aristotle, *Metaphysica* 7.6, *Works*, vol. 8.

[22] Ibid., 3, 1029b23-1030a18.

[23] Ibid., 12, 1031a15-1032a11.

[24] For *per se* and *per accidens* predication, see above pp. 13-14 and 15, and *In metaphysica* 7, lect. 3, Marietti ed.

substance which has a quality.[25] Therefore, in the case of anything to which something which does not belong to the intelligible structure of its nature can be accidental, the thing and the essence, or the supposit and the nature, differ. For in the signification of the nature is included only that which belongs to the intelligible structure of the species. But the supposit not only has what belongs to the intelligible structure of the species, but also other characteristics which are accidental to it. And therefore, the supposit is signified in the manner of a whole; however the nature or quiddity is signified as a formal part of it.

In God alone, however, no accident is found outside his essence because his being is his essence, as we said. And therefore in God supposit and nature are entirely the same. But in an angel they are not entirely the same because something outside what belongs to the intelligible structure of its species is accidental to it, both because the very being of an angel is outside its essence or nature, and some other characteristics which belong entirely to the supposit are accidental to it but not to the nature.

Therefore, to the first it must be said that not only in composites of matter and form do we find some accident outside the essence of the species itself, but also in spiritual substances which are not composed of matter and form. And therefore, in both the supposit is not entirely the same as the nature itself. However, it happens differently in each case for something is taken as an accident outside the intelligible structure of a thing in two ways. In one way because it does not enter into the definition signifying the essence of the thing but is, however, designative or determinative of some one of the essential principles. In this way *rational* is accidental to *animal* as belonging outside its definition and is, nonetheless, essentially determinative of 'animal'; hence it is essential to a man and belongs to the intelligible structure of a man. In the other way something is accidental to something because it is neither in its definition nor determinative of any of its essential principles. In this way whiteness is accidental to a man. Therefore, in both ways something which belongs outside the intelligible structure of the species is accidental to those things which are composed of matter and form. For since the intelligible structure of the human species comprehends man's composition of soul and

---

[25] Aristotle, *Categoriae* 5, 3b17-20, *Works*, vol. 1.

body, the determination of body and soul which is from this soul and this body is outside the intelligible structure of the species and is accidental to a man as a man. But it is attributable of itself to this man to whose intelligible structure it would belong, if he were defined, that he be from this soul and this body, just as it pertains to the intelligible structure of man in general that he be composed of a soul and a body. Many other characteristics outside the intelligible structure of the species which are not determinative of the essential principles are also accidental to composites of matter and form. Some characteristics outside the intelligible structure of the species which are not determinative of the essential principles are accidental to created immaterial substances, as we said. However, some characteristics which are determinative of the species' essence are not accidental to them because the very nature of the species is not individuated through matter but through itself only, from the fact that such a form is not suited to being received in any matter; whence through itself only it is not capable of multiplication nor predicable of many. But because such a substance is not its being, something outside the intelligible structure of the species is accidental to it, namely being itself and certain other characteristics which are attributed to the supposit and not to the nature. Thus in such a substance the supposit is not entirely the same as the nature.

To the second it must be said that not everything outside the intelligible structure of the species which is accidental to something is determinative of the very essence so that it is necessarily included in its intelligible structure, as we said. And therefore, although being itself does not belong to a supposit's intelligible structure, yet because it belongs to the supposit and does not belong to the nature's intelligible structure, it is clear that supposit and nature are not entirely the same in any cases in which a thing is not its being.

To that which is objected on the contrary side it must be said that in composites of matter and form also a nature is said to constitute a supposit, not because a nature is one thing and a supposit another (for this is the case according to the opinion of those who say that the nature of a species is only the form which constitutes the supposit as a whole), but because according to the manner of signifying, a nature is signified as a part for the aforesaid reason and a supposit is signified as a whole. A nature is signified as what constitutes, a supposit as what is constituted.

Parallel passages: 1 *Sent.*, d. 8, q.9, a.5, qc 2; d. 25, q.1, ad 3; 3, d. 5, q.1, a.3; *Spir. creat.*, a.5, ad 9; st 1, q. 3; 3, q. 17, a.1; cg 2, c. 55; *De pot.*, q. 7, a.4; q. 9, a.1.

* * *

QUESTION 3: Then it was asked about the time through which God moves a spiritual creature, according to Augustine.

Article: Whether the time which moves a spiritual creature and the time which measures a temporal creature are the same?

Whether the time which moves a spiritual creature is the same as the time which measures the motions of corporeal things: it seems so.

1. Because neither Augustine nor any other philosopher ascribes a diversity of times.[26] Therefore, it seems fruitless to do so.

2. Moreover, everything that exists, insofar as it exists, is one. If then there is not one time but diverse times, there will be no being, which is incoherent. Therefore, it is necessary to maintain only one time.

But to the contrary:

1. the time by which corporeal motions are measured is the numbering of the motion of the first heaven, according to the Philosopher in *Physica* 4.[27] But the time through which angels are moved does not have any relation to motion. Therefore that time is other than the time of corporeal things.

2. Moreover, nothing is common to what is perpetual and what is perishable except in name, as is said in *Metaphysica* 10.[28] But angels are perpetual, and bodies are perishable. Therefore, their times are not the same.

I answer: it must be said that, as Augustine says in *De civitate Dei* 2, there would not have been times unless there were a creature which changed something by some motion. Time follows on this change when things which are diverse and cannot exist simultaneously move and succeed one another.[29] From this what the Philosopher

---

[26] For example, see Augustine's *De Genesi ad litteram* 8, c. 20, csel 28: 259; pl 34: 388.

[27] Aristotle, *Physica* 4.12, *Works*, vol. 2.

[28] Aristotle, *Metaphysica* 10.10, *Works*, vol. 8.

[29] *De civitate Dei* 11, c. 6 contains the sense. csel 40: 519; cc 48: 326; pl 41: 321.

says in *Physica* 4 is also understood: "It is necessary to speak of time according to the intelligible structure of motion, for time is the numbering of motion according to before and after." [30] Therefore, all motions which can be measured by one measure have one time and if there are motions which cannot be measured by one measure, then necessarily their times are diverse. However, since a measure is of like kind with what is measured, as *Metaphysica* 10 says, it is clear that all that belong to one genus can have one common measure, but what belong to diverse genera cannot.[31] Now all continuous motions belong to one genus insofar as they are commensurable, and therefore they can have one common measure. For all are measured by the simplest in their genus, namely by the fastest motion of the first heaven, so there can be one common time for all continuous motions.[32] This time indeed, although it seems to belong to the genus of the numbering of discrete things, because it is the numbering of these continuous things, namely motions, it becomes also itself continuous, just as ten simply understood is something discrete but ten lengths of cloth are something continuous. However, there cannot be one common measure of discrete and continuous things since it belongs to diverse genera insofar as they are measurable. And therefore it is necessary, if there be some noncontinuous motions, that their time be other than the motion by which continuous motions are measured.

But clearly the motions of spiritual creatures, of which Augustine speaks when he says spiritual creatures are moved through time and not through place, are not continuous motions but certain discrete changes.[33] For he says that a mind is moved through time either by remembering what was forgotten, or by learning what it did not know, or by willing what it did not will. So it is clear that since time

---

[30] Aristotle, *Physica* 4.11, 219b1-4; 220a25, *Works*, vol. 2.

[31] Aristotle, *Metaphysica* 10.1, 1053a24-25, *Works*, vol. 8.

[32] According to the cosmology with which St. Thomas was familiar, there were nine concentric geocentric spheres. The outermost sphere, the first in that ordering, was called the Primum Mobile. It was followed by the sphere of the fixed stars, and that by the spheres of the planets. The Primum Mobile contained no stars. Its motion was perfect in the east-west direction and imparted a twenty-four hour motion to the stars and planets. See St. Thomas, *In metaphysica* 12, lect. 9, no. 2558, Marietti ed. Also see the note to his *Commentary on St. Paul's Epistle to the Ephesians*, by Matthew Lamb, pp. 306-309.

[33] See note 26 above.

has continuity only from motion, such time has no continuum and is different from the time of corporeal things.

Therefore, to the first it must be said that Augustine makes the difference of times understood from the very difference of the motions.

To the second it must be said that something is one in that way in which it is said to exist. For what is said to exist according to species is one in species but not in number. So it does not follow that if there are many men that the species man does not exist. And likewise it does not follow that if there are many times time does not exist.

Parallel passages: Quodlibet 10, q. 2; st 1, q. 10, a.5; *De pot.*, q. 3, a.14, ad 18; 1 *Sent.*, d. 8, q.2, a.2; d. 19, q.2, a.1; 2 *Sent.*, d. 2, q.1, a.1.

* * *

Then questions were asked concerning man: first as to the virtues, second as to sins, third as to punishments. Concerning the virtues, however, questions were asked both in relation to divine matters and human matters.

QUESTION 4: Three questions were asked with regard to virtues in relation to divine matters:
1. concerning faith, whether someone would be bound to believe a Christ who did not perform visible miracles?
2. concerning the sacrament of faith, whether the children of Jews are to be baptized when their parents are unwilling?
3. concerning tithes which are owed to ministers of the sacraments, whether someone can be excused from paying tithes because of a custom?

Article 1: Whether men ought to have believed a Christ who did not perform visible miracles?[34]

---

[34] According to a distinction made by Augustine in *Sermones de scripturis* 144.2, PL 38: 788 and *In Iohannis evangelium*, tr. 29 (on John 7:17), CC 36: 287; PL 35: 1631, and picked up by Peter Lombard in *Sent.* 3, d. 23, c.4, Quaracchi ed., 2: 656-657, there are three senses of the verb *credere* where the object is God: *credere Deo, credere Deum, credere in Deum*. These are often translated as 'believing God', 'believing in God', and 'believing unto God'. See ST 2-2, q. 2, a.2, Blackfriars ed., 31: 64-69. The Latin in this article reads *credere Christo*, translated 'to believe Christ'.

On the first we proceed as follows: it seems that men were not bound to believe a Christ who did not perform visible miracles.

1. For whoever does not do this to which he is bound, sins. But if men did not believe a Christ who did not perform miracles, they did not sin. Christ himself says in John 15:24, "If I had not done among them works which no one else did, they would not have had sin," and according to Augustine he is speaking of the sin of lack of faith.[35] Therefore, men would not have been bound to believe Christ if he had not performed miracles.

2. Moreover, only a lawmaker or someone higher than him can change the law. But Christ taught some things which seemed to pertain to the abolition of the Old Law, such as that foods do not defile a man, and that it is permissible to work on the sabbath. If, therefore, he had not proved himself to be a lawmaker, it would not have been necessary to believe him. But he could not have proved this except through miracles since many miracles had preceded the lawmaking. Therefore, it was not necessary to believe Christ unless he had performed miracles.

But to the contrary:

3. men are obligated to believe the first truth more than visible signs. But even though Christ had not performed miracles, he himself, being the true God, was the first truth. Therefore, even if he had not performed miracles, it was still necessary to believe him.

4. Moreover, the grace of union is greater than the grace which sanctifies.[36] But miracles do not sufficiently prove a sanctifying grace because, as Matthew 7:22 says to those who say to Christ at judgment, "Lord, we did many wonderful things in your name," it will be answered, "I did not know you." Therefore, much less do miracles suffice to prove a grace of union. If then men were not bound to believe Christ without miracles, even when miracles were performed they were not bound to believe the one who said he was God, which is clearly false.

---

[35] Augustine, *In Iohannis evangelium*, tr. 91 (on John 15:24), cc 36: 553; pl 35: 1860, no. 1.

[36] The grace of union is that by which Christ is a natural son of the Father. Sanctifying grace, or *gratia gratum faciens*, is that by which someone is pleasing to God; it is the grace which unites a man to God. See st 1-2, q. 111, a.1, Blackfriars ed., 30: 124-129.

I answer: it must be stated that no one is bound to what is above his powers except in the manner in which it is possible for him. However, believing is above man's natural power. Hence it arises from a gift of God, according to what the Apostle says in Ephesians 2:8, "For by grace you are saved through faith not from yourselves for it is the gift of God," and in Philippians 1:29, "It is given you not only to believe in him but to suffer for him as well." A man, therefore, is bound to believe insofar as he is helped by God to believe.

Now God helps someone to believe in three ways. First through an inner calling, concerning which John 6:45 says, "Everyone who has heard and learned from the Father comes to me," and Romans 8:30 says, "Whom he predestined, these also he called." Second through outer teaching and preaching, according to the Apostle in Romans 10:17, "Faith comes from hearing, hearing however through the word of Christ." Third through outer miracles, whence 1 Cor. 14:22 says that signs are given to those lacking faith in order that they may be roused to faith through them. If Christ had not performed visible miracles, however, there still remained other ways of drawing to faith to which men would be bound to give assent. For men were bound to believe the authority of the law and the prophets. They were also bound not to resist an inner calling, as Isaiah 50:5 says concerning himself, "The Lord God opened my ear, but I did not resist nor turn away back," (as Acts 7:51 says concerning some, "You always resist the Holy Spirit").

Therefore, to the first it must be said that among those works which Christ performed among men, we should also count the inner calling by which he drew some people. Gregory says in a homily that Christ through compassion drew Mary Magdalene from within whom he also received through gentleness without.[37] We should also count his teaching since he himself also says (John 15:22), "If I had not come and spoken to them they had had no sin."

To the second it must be said that Christ was able to show himself to be a lawmaker, not only by performing visible miracles, but also through the authority of scripture and through inner inspiration.

To the third it must be said that the inner inspiration by which Christ could manifest himself without outer miracles pertains to the power of the first truth which illuminates and teaches man inwardly.

[37] Gregory the Great, *Homiliae in evangelia* 2, Hom. 33, PL 76: 1239-1240, no. 1.

To the fourth it must be said that visible miracles are performed by divine power in order to strengthen the virtue of faith, whence Mark 16:20 says concerning the apostles that "they preached everywhere, the Lord working with them and confirming the words with signs that followed." However, miracles are not always performed in order to demonstrate the grace of him through whom they are performed. And therefore it can happen that someone without the grace which sanctifies may perform miracles. But it cannot happen that someone announcing a false doctrine should perform a true miracle which can only be performed by divine power, for thus God would be a witness to falsehood, which is impossible. Therefore, when Christ called himself the son of God and equal to God, the miracles which he performed confirmed his teaching, and Christ was shown to be God through them. However Peter, although he performed the same or greater miracles, was not proved to be God but through them also Christ was proved to be God because Peter did not teach that he himself, but rather Jesus Christ, was God.

Parallel passages: ST 3, q. 43, a.4; *In Ioann.*, c. 15, lectio 5.

Article 2: Whether the children of Jews should be baptized when their parents are unwilling?[38]

On the second we proceed as follows: it seems that the children of Jews should be baptized when their parents are unwilling for them to be.

1. For the marriage bond is greater than the right of parental power because parental power can be dissolved by man when a child is emancipated, but the marriage bond cannot be dissolved by man, according to Matthew 19:6, "Let man not separate whom God has joined together." The marriage bond is dissolved because of lack of belief, for the Apostle says in 1 Cor. 7:15, "Because if an unbeliever departs, let him depart, for a brother or a sister is not bound in such cases," and canon law says that if an unbelieving spouse does not want to cohabit with the other, without affront to the creator, then the other spouse is not obligated to cohabit with him or her."[39]

---

[38] The text of this article is almost identical with that of ST 2-2, q. 10, a.12, Blackfriars ed., vol. 32, and with parts of ST 3, q. 68, a.10, Blackfriars ed., vol. 57.

[39] Gratian, *Decretum* 2, C. 28, q.1, c.4 and q.2, c.2, *Corpus iuris canonici* 1: 936 and 947; PL 187: 1415 and 1428-1429.

Therefore, much more is the right of parental power removed because of lack of belief. So then, unbelieving Jews do not have the right of parental power over their children. Their children can therefore be baptized when the parents are unwilling.

2. Moreover, we ought more to aid men against the danger of eternal death than against the danger of temporal death. But if someone saw a man in danger of temporal death and did not aid him, he would sin. So since the children of Jews and other unbelievers are in danger of eternal death if they are left to their parents who instruct them in their lack of belief, it seems that they should be removed from them and baptized and instructed in the faith.

3. Moreover, slaves' children are slaves and in the power of their lords. But Jews are slaves of kings and princes, therefore so are their children, hence kings and princes have the power to do what they want concerning the children of Jews. Therefore, there would be no harm if they were baptized when their parents are unwilling.

4. Further, any man belongs more to God from whom he has his soul than to his parent of the flesh from whom he has his body. So it is not unjust if the children of Jews be removed from their parents of the flesh and consecrated to God through baptism.

5. Further, baptism is more efficacious for salvation than is preaching because through baptism the stain of sin and guilt of punishment are removed at once, and the door of heaven is opened. But if danger follows from lack of preaching it is imputed to him who did not preach, as is said in Ezekiel 3:18 and 33:6 concerning the man who saw the sword coming and did not sound the trumpet. Therefore, if the children of Jews are damned because of lack of baptism, all the more is it imputed as a sin to those who could baptize and did not.

But to the contrary: harm must be done to no one. Now it would harm the Jews if their children were baptized when they were unwilling, because they would lose the right of parental power over their children as soon as the children joined the believers. Therefore, they must not be baptized when their parents are unwilling.

I answer: it must be said that the custom of the Church has the greatest authority which must always be followed in all things, because even the very teaching of the catholic theologians has authority from the Church. Hence we should stand more on the Church's custom than on the authority of Augustine or Jerome or any teacher. Now the Church never had the practice of baptizing the children of Jews when their parents were unwilling, although in past times there were many very powerful catholic princes such as Constantine, Theodosius, and many others with whom very holy bishops were friendly, such as Silvester with Constantine, and Ambrose with Theodosius.[40] These princes would not have neglected to obtain [the power] from them if this were harmonious with reason. And therefore it seems dangerous to assert anew, contrary to the custom so far observed in the Church, that the children of Jews may be baptized when their parents are unwilling.

There are two reasons for this. One is because of the danger to the faith. For if children who do not yet have the use of reason undertake baptism, later when they arrive at adulthood they may easily be led by their parents to relinquish what they undertook when ignorant, and this might be turned to the detriment of the faith. The other reason is that it is contrary to natural justice. For a child naturally belongs to his parents. At first he is not distinguished from his parent physically so long as he is contained in his mother's womb. Later, after he passes out of the womb and before he has the use of free choice, he is in the care of his parents as in a kind of spiritual womb. For as long as a child does not have the use of reason he does not differ from a nonrational animal in what he does. So, just as a cow or a horse belongs by civil law or the law of the people to the owner so that he may use it when he wants as his own instrument, so according to natural law a child before he has the use of reason is under his parents' care.[41] It would then be against natural justice if a

---

[40] St. Ambrose, 339-397, was bishop of Milan at a time when that city was the capital of the western Roman Empire. He was thus in close touch with the emperors in the West. One of these was Theodosius, ruling 379-395, whom St. Ambrose had occasion to excommunicate as a result of the former's massacre at Thessalonica in 390. Constantine was Roman emperor from 306 to 337. He supposedly converted to Christianity in 312. The spurious Donation of Constantine gave Pope Sylvester I (ruled 314-335) supreme authority over Europe, and allegedly placed the pope even above the emperors. See *The New Catholic Encyclopedia*, articles on "St. Ambrose," by M. R. P. McGuire, vol. 1, pp. 372-375, and on the "Donation of Constantine," by F. X. Murphy, vol. 4.

[41] In sᴛ 1-2, q. 91, Blackfriars ed., 28: 18-39, St. Thomas describes the following types of law. Eternal law is the conception of things in the divine reason. Natural law is a participation in eternal law; it is the eternal law imprinted on creatures, giving them their proper inclinations and acts. Human law, also called positive law, results

child before he had the use of free choice were taken away from his parents' care or if something were ordered concerning him against his parents' will. However, after he begins to have the use of free choice he begins to be his own person and can provide for himself with regard to those things which pertain to divine or natural law. And then he should be led to the faith, not by compulsion but by persuasion, and he can also consent to the faith and be baptized when his parents are unwilling – not, however, before he has the use of reason.

Hence it is said of the children of parents in ancient times that they were saved in their parents' faith, through which we are given to understand that it is up to the parents to provide for their children's salvation, especially before they have the use of reason.

Therefore, to the first it must be stated that in the marriage bond each spouse has the use of free choice and each can assent to the faith when the other is unwilling. But this is not so with a child before he has the use of reason. The likeness holds after he has the use of reason, if he wants to be converted.

To the second it must be stated that no one must be taken away from temporal death against the order of the civil law. For example if someone is condemned to death by its judge, no one ought to rescue him violently. Neither then ought anyone violate the order of natural law by which a child is under his parents' care in order to free him from the danger of eternal death.

To the third it must be said that the Jews are slaves of princes by a civil servitude which does not exclude the order of natural or divine law.

To the fourth it must be said that man is ordered to God through reason through which he can know God. So a child before he has the use of reason is ordered to God by a natural order through the reason of his parents to whose care he is naturally subject. And divine things must be done concerning him according to their disposition.

To the fifth it must be said that the danger following from neglected preaching threatens only him to whom the duty of preaching was

---

from men making particular determinations about particular matters on the basis of the precepts of natural law. Divine law is that given by God to direct men to their supernatural end, e.g., the Old and New Laws.

committed. Hence in Ezekiel 33:7 he prefaces, "I gave you a watchman for the children of Israel." However, with regard to the children of unbelievers, it is up to the parents to provide the sacraments of salvation. So the danger threatens them if their little ones suffer any harm to salvation because of being deprived of the sacraments.

Parallel passages: ST 2-2, q. 10, a.12; 3, q. 68, a.10.

Article 3: Whether some people can be excused from the law of paying tithes because of a custom?

On the third we proceed as follows: it seems that some people are excused from the law of paying tithes because of a custom. For there is more reason to receive tithes than there is not to give them. But because of a custom, in some lands some soldiers receive tithes and this is tolerated by the Church. Therefore, all the more are some people excused from paying tithes because of a custom, nor are they obligated to pay them.

But to the contrary: divine law is not abolished because a custom is lacking, but tithes are owed because of a divine law, therefore the law requiring payment of tithes is not abolished through lack of a custom. Men are then bound to pay tithes, a contrary custom notwithstanding.

I answer: it must be said that those things which pertain to positive law are abolished through lack of a custom. But no lack of a custom can abolish those things which are from natural or divine law, for no lack of a custom can make it permissible to steal or commit adultery. Therefore, in connection with the proposed question we must consider whether giving tithes pertains to divine law or to positive human law.

Now divine law is contained in the New and Old Testaments. In the New Testament, no precept seems to be given concerning payment of tithes, either in evangelic or apostolic teaching. For what Matthew 23:23 says concerning the payment of tithes, "It was necessary to do these and not to omit those," and what the Pharisee says in Luke 18:12, "I give tithes of all that I possess," seem to pertain to the condition of the Old Testament rather than to impose a form of observance of the New Testament.

In the Old Testament, however, there was a threefold genus of precepts. Some were moral precepts, some judicial, some ceremonial. Moral precepts were engrafted in the natural reason to which men are obligated at all times – "Honor your father and mother," "Do not commit adultery," "Do not steal," and the like. Judicial precepts are those through which trials were conducted, e.g., if someone steals one sheep he should return four, and such precepts are not engrafted in natural reason for natural reason does not hold that one who steals a sheep should return four rather than three or five, but rather a moral precept is determined through such precepts. Natural reason holds that one who steals ought to be punished, but that he be punished by such and such a punishment is determined through a judicial precept. Moreover, the ceremonial precepts of the Old Law are those which pertain to the observance of divine worship and were ordained to symbolize something future, just as the sacrifice of the paschal lamb symbolized the killing of Christ.

Therefore, we must consider whether the precept concerning the payment of tithes is moral, judicial, or ceremonial. For if it is moral, all are bound to it in all times, a contrary custom notwithstanding. But this does not seem to be the case because natural reason does not dictate that a man should give a tenth part to the ministers of God rather than an eleventh or a ninth part of the fruit of his labor. If it is a judicial precept, men are not bound to give tithes, just as all are not bound to judge according to the judgments written in the Old Law because those judicial precepts were specially given to those people with their conditions taken into account, for they do not settle things the same way for all. However, if it is a ceremonial precept it not only would not obligate but its observance would even lead to sin, for if someone sacrificed a paschal lamb he would sin because the symbols ceased after the coming of the Truth.

Therefore, we must say, as past teachers have done, that some precepts of the law are purely moral, such as "Do not kill," "Do not steal." Some are purely ceremonial such as the sacrifice of a paschal lamb and circumcision. And some are intermediate, moral in a way and ceremonial in a way, as the precept concerning the observation of the sabbath is moral as it concerns the allotment of a time of rest for freedom for divine matters, because natural reason maintains this; but the allotment of the seventh day is due to God's determination for the sake of some symbol; hence this is a ceremonial precept.

So then the precept concerning the payment of tithes is indeed in some way a moral one in providing that they who are free for divine obedience for the whole people's sake may be supported by the people's stipends as also they who serve in other offices of the state are supported by the whole people. And this precept is proposed in the New Testament in this manner, for the Lord says in Matthew 10:10, "The worker is worthy of his food," and the Apostle says in 1 Cor. 9:14, "The Lord ordained that they who preach the Gospel live from the Gospel, and they who serve the altar live from the altar." But a determined amount of tithes does not pertain to natural law nor is the precept a moral one, but it is ceremonial inasmuch as it is related to symbolizing something about Christ, or it is even judicial according to its suitability for that people among whom, because there was a multitude of ministers, there was need for such taxation for the support of God's ministers.[42]

Therefore, this common law, to provide for the ministers of God in the necessities of life, is from divine law like a moral precept, and from natural law. However, it is up to any prince who can establish laws to determine the natural common law through a positive law, for positive law is nothing but the determination of natural law. (For example, natural law holds that a malefactor should be punished, but that he be punished by a particular punishment is determined through a positive law). Therefore, because the Church has the power of establishing law in matters which pertain to the worship of God, the amount of what the people are to give the ministers of God could be determined by Church statute. And in order that there might be some agreement of the Old and New Testaments, the Church decreed that the taxation of the Old Testament be kept also in the New. Hence all are obliged to tithes willy nilly. The Church could, however, decree, if there were cause, either a greater or a lesser amount, e.g., that an eighth be given, or a twelfth, as well as that a tenth be given.

So no contrary custom frees a man from the obligation of paying tithes because this obligation is founded on divine and natural law.

---

[42] This is explained more fully in sт 2-2, q. 87, a.1, Blackfriars ed., 39: 140-143. A tenth is something ceremonial in that it signifies a future perfection, for ten is a perfect number; it is judicial also in the sense that it took into consideration the conditions of the twelve tribes of Israel, eleven of which gave a tenth part of what they had to the Levite tribe so that the members of that tribe, who devoted themselves to divine ministries (Num. 18:21), might live more honorably.

Hence men are always bound to pay tithes if the Church demands, a contrary custom notwithstanding. And in the lands in which there is a custom that tithes be paid, the custom itself, as it were, demands the tithes, hence he who would not pay would sin. But in lands in which it is not the common custom that tithes be given and the Church does not require them, the Church seems to renounce them so long as it ignores them. And therefore, men in those lands do not sin in not giving tithes for it would be difficult to say that all the men of Italy and the Eastern parts who do not pay tithes would be damned.

And we can get such an argument from the Apostle who, when the necessities of life were due him by those to whom he preached, however did not take them nor did they sin who did not give to him, otherwise he had done wrongly by them in not taking them, especially since he himself says in Acts 20:27, "I have not evaded declaring to you every counsel of God." Therefore, the Apostle did not demand what was due him lest some hindrance be given to the Gospel, as he himself says there. Hence the rectors of the churches would not do well if they demanded tithes in those lands in which it is not the custom for them to be given, if they believed with probability that they would give rise to a scandal from doing so.

Therefore, to that which is objected on the contrary side it must be said that soldiers who receive tithes in some lands do not have the right to do so for this right is a spiritual one owed the ministers of God; hence it does not fall on a lay person. But those temporal things which are demanded by the law are given some soldiers from a concession of the Church because of a service they performed for the Church; in the same way the Church can renounce those fruits of labor which are due as tithes but it does not renounce the right of demanding tithes nor remove the debt of paying them.

Parallel passages: Quodlibet 6, q. 5, a.4; *In Matth.*, c. 23; *Ad Hebr.*, c. 7, lects. 1, 2; ST 2-2, q. 87, a.1.

* * *

QUESTION 5: Then it was asked concerning these things which pertain to the virtues in relation to human affairs. And two questions were asked:
1. whether a child is bound to obey his parents of the flesh in indifferent matters?
2. whether a seller is bound to tell a buyer a defect in an item sold?

Article 1: Whether a child is bound to obey his parents of the flesh in everything?

On the first we proceed as follows: it seems that a child is bound to obey his parents of the flesh in everything.

1. For it is said in Deuteronomy 21:18-21, if a man begat an obstinate and shameless son who does not hear his mother's or father's command, the people of the city should strike him down with stones. Such a punishment would not be inflicted unless he sinned gravely by not obeying, so children are bound to obey their parents of the flesh in all things.

2. Moreover, the Apostle says in Colossians 3:21, "Children, obey your parents in all matters."

3. Further, although affirmative moral precepts do not obligate for all times, it is yet never permissible to act contrary to them. But there is an affirmative moral precept concerning honoring one's parents. Therefore it is not permissible to be irreverent to a parent, which would be the case if his command were not obeyed. Hence a child is bound to obey his parents in all things.

But to the contrary: spiritual parents must not be obeyed less but more than parents of the flesh, as the Apostle maintains in Hebrews 12:9. But subordinates are not bound to obey spiritual parents in indifferent matters, for religious who profess obedience are only bound to obey their prelates in those matters which are according to the Rule, as Bernard says in *De dispensatione et praecepto*.[43] Therefore, neither are children bound to obey their parents of the flesh in indifferent matters.

I answer: it must be said that, since obedience is due a superior, the duty of obedience is extended as far as his authority. Now a father of the flesh first has authority over a child with regard to domestic life, for the head of the family is related to the home as a king to a realm; hence just as the king's subjects are bound to obey him in those matters which pertain to the government of the realm, so are children and other domestic members bound to obey the head of the family in those matters which pertain to the management of the home. The father has authority secondly with regard to moral instruction. Hence

---

[43] Bernard of Clairvaux, *Tractatus de praecepto*, c. 4, nos. 9-10, c. 5, no. 11, *Opera* 3: 259-261, esp. 260, lines 15-18; PL 182: 865-867.

the Apostle says in Hebrews 12:9, "Indeed we had fathers of the flesh who taught us and we revered them." For the father owes the child not only upbringing but also instruction, as the Philosopher says.[44] In these areas then the child is bound to obey his father of flesh, and not in others.

Therefore to the first it must be said that Moses speaks there of the paternal command which pertains to moral instruction, so in the same place it is said, "He despises to hear our counsels, he has leisure to devote himself to dissipation and reveling and riotous living." (Deut. 21:20)

To the second it must be said that the Apostle says parents must be obeyed in all matters to which their authority extends.

To the third it must be said he does not exhibit irreverence to one who gives rules if he does not obey him in those matters in which he is not bound to obey.

Parallel passages: ST 2-2, q. 104, a.5; *In Ioann.*, c. 2, lect. 1; *Ad Rom.*, c. 13, lect. 1; *Ad Tit.*, c. 3, lect. 1.

Article 2: Whether a seller is bound to tell a buyer about a defect in an item sold?

On the second we proceed as follows: it seems that a seller is not bound to tell a buyer about a defect in an item sold.

1. Because according to civil laws, buyer and seller can deceive each other. But there could be no deception if a seller were bound to tell a buyer about a defect in an item sold. Therefore, he is not bound to do so.

2. But it was objected that the laws do not speak with regard to the court of conscience, and that we speak now according to a contentious court. To the contrary: according to the Philosopher in *Ethica* 2, the lawmaker's intention is to make good citizens.[45] Therefore, what is permissible according to the laws is not contrary to virtue and so also is not contrary to conscience.

But to the contrary:

1. he is so obligated because according to civil laws, if someone sells a sickly animal he is obligated with respect to the defect. Hence he is bound to tell a buyer about the defect.

[44] Aristotle, *Ethica nicomachea* 8.12, 1161a16, *Works*, vol. 9.
[45] Ibid., 2.1, 1103b3-5.

2. Moreover, Tully says in *De officiis* that it is part of a good man's duty to tell a buyer the reason for which a thing might be sold at a lower price.[46] Now a defect in an item sold is such a reason, so a seller is bound to tell a buyer about a defect in an item sold.

I answer: it must be said that something pertains to the good of men to which men are not however bound, as it pertains to the good of men that one give his goods liberally to a friend although he is not bound to this. And something pertains to the good of men to which one is bound, namely that one pay someone what is just, for it is an act of justice that what is owed someone be paid him. And therefore, every seller is bound to make a just sale but not to make a liberal sale by giving up some of the just price.

Now justice is a kind of equality, as is said in *Ethica* 5.[47] There is therefore a just sale when the price received by the seller is equivalent to the thing sold, but there is an unjust sale if it is not equivalent but he receives more. So if a defect in the thing sold makes the thing worth less than the price imposed by the seller, the sale will be unjust; hence he sins in hiding the defect. However, if it does not make the thing worth less than the price imposed, perhaps because the seller imposes a lower price because of the defect, then he does not sin in being silent about the defect because the sale is not unjust. And perhaps it would be detrimental to him if he did tell because the buyer would want to have the thing for an even lower price than it was worth. But he would act liberally if he held loss to himself in contempt in order that he might satisfy another person's will, although he is not bound to do this.

Therefore, to the first it must be said that that statement of the law does not mean that it is permissible for a simple seller to deceive a buyer and conversely. But something is said to be permissible according to the law when it is not punished through the law, as a petition for divorce was permitted according to the Old Law.

To the second it must be said that the law's precepts are capable of leading to perfect virtue. Now acts of perfect virtue do not fall under a precept of human law but human law prohibits some more serious sins in order that gradually men, having been drawn back from evils,

---

[46] Cicero, *De officiis* 3, 15, no. 61, ed. and transl. W. Miller (Cambridge, Mass., 1913), no. 61.

[47] Aristotle, *Ethica nicomachea* 5.2 and 3, 1131a10-30, *Works*, vol. 9.

may be conducted to virtue through their own persons. However, it permits some lesser sins and does not inflict punishment on them because the multitude of men is certainly not found without them, and among such is the deception between buyers and sellers for there are a great many who want to buy cheap and sell dear, as Augustine says in *De trinitate*.[48]

Indeed to that which first is objected on the contrary side, it must be said that we must understand that to be the case when the disease of the beast makes it worth less than the price for which it is sold.

To the second it must be said that Tully says that a good man is not silent concerning a defect of an item sold because deceiving someone does not pertain to the good of men. But it is not deception if what he is silent about with regard to the thing sold does not make the thing worth less than the price he receives for it.

Parallel passage: ST 2-2, q. 77, a.3.

* * *

QUESTION 6: Then two questions were asked about sins:
　　　　1. whether it is a sin to seek a ruling office?
　　　　2. whether it is a sin for a preacher to have his eye on temporal matters?

Article 1: Whether it is a sin to seek a ruling office?

On the first we proceed as follows: it seems that it is a sin to seek a ruling office.

1. For it does not seem that we can seek without sin that which existed only in the state of corrupted nature and not in the state of innocence. Now ruling positions did not exist in the latter state but began to exist after the first sin when it was said to woman in Genesis 3:16, "You will be under the man's power." Therefore, it is a sin to seek a higher office.

2. Moreover, desire seems to concern those things which pertain to the state of future glory. Now in the future all ruling positions will cease, as the *Glossa* on 1 Cor. 15:24 says.[49] Therefore, it is a sin to seek a ruling office.

---

[48] Augustine, *De trinitate* 13, c.3, ed. W. J. Moutain, CC 50A: 388 (Turnholti, 1968); PL 42: 1018.

[49] *Glossa ordinaria* (1 Ad Corinth., Cap. 15), 6: 58. Also Peter Lombard, *Collectanea* on 1 Cor. 15:24, PL 191: 1679.

But to the contrary: 1 Timothy 5:17 says, "Let elders who rule well be held worthy of a double honor." But it is not a sin to seek that for which honor is due when it is due only for virtue. Hence it is not a sin to seek a ruling office.

I answer: it must be said that Augustine solves this question in *De civitate Dei* 19 where he says that a ruling office, without which the people cannot be governed, is not fittingly sought even if it be administered as is fitting, because he who seeks a ruling office is either proud or unjust.[50] Now it is a matter of injustice for someone to want to take more honor for himself, either power or other goods, unless he is worthy of greater things, as is said in *Ethica* 5, 3, but it is a matter of pride and presumption for someone to esteem himself to be more worthy for a ruling office than all those over whom he takes office.[51] Hence clearly whoever seeks a ruling office is either unjust or proud. And therefore, no one ought to succeed to a ruling office by his desire, but only by God's judgment, according to what the Apostle says in Hebrews 5:4, "No one takes honor for himself except the one who is called by God as Aaron was." But anyone is permitted to desire himself to be worthy of a ruling office, or to desire the works of a good prelate for which honor is due.

Therefore, the response to the last argument is clear.

Indeed the first two arguments do not conclude rightly because even those things which did not exist in the state of innocence nor will exist in the state of glory can be permissibly sought, such as being subject to another, repentance, and the like (although ruling offices in some sense existed in the state of innocence and will exist in the state of glory as far as superiority of degree, and government or rule are concerned, but not as far as compulsory servitude is concerned).

Parallel passages: Quodlibet 6, q. 11, a.2; 12, q. 11, a.3; *De perfect. vitae spirit.*, c. 19; 1 *Tim.*, c. 3, lect. 1.

Article 2: Whether it is a sin for a preacher to have his eye on temporal matters?

On the second we proceeded as follows: it seems that it is a sin for a preacher to have his eye on temporal matters. For it is said in Luke 12:31, "Seek first the kingdom of God," on which the *Glossa* says,

---

[50] Augustine, *De civitate Dei* 19, c.19, CSEL 40: 407; CC 48: 686; PL 41: 647.

[51] Aristotle, *Ethica nicomachea* 5.13, 1131a25-30, *Works*, vol. 9.

"i.e., eternal goods," "and all these will be added to you," to which the *Glossa* adds, "even to those not seeking them." [52] Therefore, it is not permissible for a preacher to have his eye on temporal matters.

But to the contrary: 1 Cor. 9:10 says, "He who plows ought to plow in hope," to which the *Glossa* adds, "of temporal stipends." [53] So it is permissible for a preacher, concerning whom it speaks there, to have his eye on temporal matters.

I answer: it must be said that having an eye on earthly things happens in two ways. In one way it happens with regard to payment or reward, and in this way it is not permissible for a preacher to have his eye on earthly things because he would then make the Gospel venal. In the other way it happens with regard to the stipends necessary to support life, and in this way it is permissible for a preacher to have his eye on earthly things. Hence on 1 Timothy 5:17, "Let the elders that rule, etc.," Augustine's gloss says, "It is a matter of necessity to take the means of living, it is a matter of charity to supply them. However, the Gospel is not venal because of those who do, for if they so sell, they sell a great thing cheaply. Therefore, let them take the necessities of life from the people, and the reward of dispensation from the Lord." [54]

And through this the response to the objections is clear.

Parallel passages: sᴛ 2-2, q. 100, a.3, ad 2; 4 *Sent.*, d. 25, q.3, a.2, qc 2, ad 4; *Ad Rom.*, c. 10, lect. 2.

The question that was asked concerns the punishments of sins – first with regard to the punishments themselves, second with regard to the remission of punishments.

* * *

Qᴜᴇsᴛɪᴏɴ 7: Two questions were asked concerning punishments themselves:

  1. whether a separated soul can be acted upon by corporeal fire?

---

[52] *Glossa interlinearis* (Lucae, Cap. 12), 5: 158; *Glossa ordinaria* (Lucae, Cap. 12), 5: 158.

[53] *Glossa ordinaria* of Strabo, ᴘʟ 114: 397; *Glossa interlinearis* (1 Ad Corinth. 9), 6: 45b.

[54] Augustine, *Sermones de vetere testamento* 46 ("De pastoribus"), no. 5, ed. C. Lambot, cc 41: 532-533, lines 110-115 (Turnholti, 1961); ᴘʟ 38: 273. *Glossa ordinaria* (1 Ad Timotheum, Cap. 5), 6: 121b.

2. whether one of two individuals worthy of the same punishment lingers longer in Purgatory than the other?

Article 1: Whether a separated soul can be acted upon by corporeal fire?

On the first we proceed as follows: it seems that a soul separated from the body cannot be acted upon by corporeal fire.

1. For according to the Philosopher, things that do not touch each other do not act upon each other.[55] Now corporeal fire does not touch a soul separated from the body since it does not have corporeal boundaries; however, things that touch each other have their boundaries together. Hence a separated soul is not acted upon by corporeal fire.

2. Moreover, those things that are acted upon by each other can be converted into each other. But the soul cannot be converted into corporeal fire nor conversely, so the soul cannot be acted upon by corporeal fire.

3. Moreover, Bernard says that nothing burns in hell except the proper will.[56] But the proper will, since it is something spiritual, cannot be the matter of corporeal fire. Therefore, a soul separated from the body cannot be acted upon by corporeal fire.

But to the contrary: it says in Isaiah 66:24, "Neither shall their fire be quenched."

I answer: it must be said that to be acted upon is spoken of in many ways. In the general sense, to be acted upon is the same as to receive, inasmuch as feeling and understanding are cases of being acted upon. And in this way a soul conjoined to a body is acted upon by corporeal

---

[55] Aristotle, *De generatione et corruptione* 1.6, *Works*, vol. 2.

[56] Bernard of Clairvaux, *Sermones in resurrectione Domini* 3.3, PL 183: 286-289; *Opera* 5: 105, esp. lines 15-16, and *Tractatus de gratia et libero arbitrio* 9, nos. 30, 31, PL 182: 1017-1018; *Opera* 3: 187-188. Bernard distinguishes two types of will, the common and the proper (or self) will. The common will is charity – it is common to God and men. The proper will is one's own will alone. Men have the latter sort of will when they will not for the honor of God nor for their brothers but simply for self-satisfaction. See Étienne Gilson, *La théologie mystique de saint Bernard* (Paris, 1934), pp. 73-74. The damned are eternally fixed in their proper wills and thus they are cut off from divine beatitude and are in eternal misery, Gilson, pp. 106-107.

things in sensing and understanding them, but whether it can be acted upon by corporeal things in this way when separated from the body is another question, because some say that the soul separated from the body, and even an angel, can receive cognition from sensible things.[57] But even if this opinion were true, to be acted upon by sensing and understanding is to be perfected and not to be punished, unless perhaps accidentally inasmuch as what is sensed or understood is repugnant to the will. But sensing and understanding considered in themselves are not punitive. In the proper sense, being acted upon is an opposition of agent to patient, as we are said to be acted upon when something happens to us which is contrary to our nature or will. Weakness and sadness are said to be cases of being acted upon in this sense. And indeed to be acted upon in this sense can occur in two ways. It can occur through the receiving of a contrary form, as water is acted upon by fire inasmuch as fire heats it and consequently water's natural quality is lessened. In this way a separated soul cannot be acted upon by corporeal fire because it cannot be heated or dried nor be changed according to any form or quality of corporeal fire. In the other way we say that all that is in any way kept from its proper impetus or inclination is acted upon, as we say a falling stone is acted upon when it is impeded in such a way that it cannot fall down, and as we say a man is acted upon when he is detained or bound so that he cannot go where he wants. And in this way, through a kind of binding the soul is acted upon by corporeal fire as Augustine says in *De civitate Dei* 21.[58] It is not against nature for a spirit to be bound to a body since we see the soul naturally bound to the body to give it life. Demons also, through necromancy, are bound by the power of higher demons to some images or other things. All the more then can spirits be bound to corporeal fire by means of divine power, not so as to give life but so as to receive punishment, as Augustine says.[59]

---

[57] This may be the position of Gregory the Great, *Dialogorum libri 4*, 4, PL 77: 368, no. 29.

[58] Augustine, *De civitate Dei* 21, c. 10, CSEL 40: 537-539; CC 48: 775-776; PL 41: 724-725.

[59] Ibid. See also St. Thomas, *Compendium theologiae*, c. 180, Leonine ed., vol. 42. God can bind spiritual substances to bodies like hell-fire. The fire can be spiritual, and then the distress is due to the soul's awareness that it is bound to a lower creature when it is imprisoned by the fire. Or the fire can be corporeal, and then the soul experiences it.

But because what has lesser power cannot by its power bind that which has greater power, no body can bind a spirit, which has greater power, except by means of some higher power. And because of this it is said that corporeal fire acts upon a separated soul, not by its own power but insofar as it is an instrument of divine vindicating justice.

Therefore, to the first it must be said that fire touches the soul, not indeed by a mathematical contact which is understood according to quantitative boundaries, but rather by contact of a power not its own but which it has insofar as it is an instrument of divine justice.

To the second it must be said that that argument proceeds concerning the being acted upon which comes through the reception of a contrary form.

To the third it must be said that the proper will is said to burn in hell because it deserves the heat.

Parallel passages: Quodlibet 3, q. 10, a.1; 7, q. 5, a.3; ST 1, q. 64, a.4, ad 1; CG 4, c. 90; *Quaest. de anima*, q. 6, ad 7; q. 21; *Spir. creat.*, a.1, ad 20; *De ver.*, q. 26, a.1; *Comp. theol.*, c. 180.

Article 2: Whether one of two persons who are worthy of the same punishment lingers longer in Purgatory than the other?

On the second we proceeded as follows: it seems that one of two persons who are deserving of equal punishment cannot be freed from Purgatory more quickly than the other.

1. For judgment after death is not of man but of God who judges according to the truth, as is said in Romans 2:2. But God would judge against the truth if a more severe punishment for the senses were inflicted on one of them who are deserving of equal punishment than on the other. Now delay of glory is a greater punishment than the painfulness of punishment for the senses because, as Chrysostom says in *Super Matth.*, to be cut off from the divine vision is a greater punishment than any punishment for the senses.[60] Therefore, one of those persons who are deserving of equal punishment cannot suffer a greater delay of glory than the other who is more quickly freed.

---

[60] John Chrysostom, *Commentarius in sanctum Matthaeum evangelistam*, Homily 23, PG 57: 317. There are two kinds of punishment, the lack of divine vision due for the sin of aversion and involving the loss of the infinite good, and punishment for the senses due for an inordinate conversion to mutable goods. See ST 2-2, q. 79, a.4, Blackfriars ed., vol. 38.

2. Further, according to Augustine something is called evil because it harms and it harms because it removes a good.[61] Delay of glory, however, removes a greater good, namely an uncreated good, so it is a greater evil. And so the same as in argument 1.

But to the contrary:

3. the Master says in 4 *Sent.*, d. 45, that he for whom many prayers are said is freed from Purgatory's punishments more quickly.[62] However, it happens that more prayers are said for one of them who are deserving of equal punishment than for the other. So one will be freed more quickly.

4. Moreover, at the end of the world are found some who have sins needing cleansing, whose delay from glory will not be as long as that of those who bring such sins to Purgatory, because the delay between death and resurrection will be short, as Augustine says.[63] Hence for the same reason now also, one of those who bring equal sins can be delayed less from glory than the other and so he will be more quickly freed from the punishments.

I answer: it must be said that this question is founded on the power of prayers – whether prayers made for someone avail only for that person for whose liberation they are made, or for others also. Concerning this matter some said that they do not avail more for the former than for the others; rather they perhaps avail more for the others if these are better disposed to receive the power of the prayers.[64] And they use an example: it is as if a candle lit in a home for a wealthy man who is blind gives light to all living in the house and perhaps gives more light to others if they have clearer vision. According to this opinion, one of two persons who are detained in Purgatory because of equal faults cannot be freed more quickly than the other.

But I do not regard this opinion as true because the prayer of one avails for another for two reasons. It avails in one way because of the unity of charity, because all who are in charity are like one body and

[61] Augustine, *Enchiridion*, c. 12, cc 46: 54; pl 40: 237.

[62] Peter Lombard, *Sent.* 4, d. 45, Quaracchi ed., 2: 1005-1009; pl 192: 948-949.

[63] Augustine, *Sermones ad populum (de diversis)* 362 ("De resurrectione mortuorum"), c. 17, pl 39: 1624-1625.

[64] See Prepositinus, *Summa* 1.4, *Opera, Revue des sciences philosophiques et théologiques* (Kain, 1927 –) ("De parvulis qui decedunt baptizati").

just as the hand is devoted to the whole body and likewise to any member of the body, so the good of one redounds to all. Thus any good done by someone avails anyone who is in charity, according to Psalm 119 (118):63, "I am the companion of all who fear you and of those who keep your commandments." It avails also in another way if someone's act is transferred to another through his intention, for example if someone pays a debt for another person, because there is the same result as if that one had paid it for himself. So in the first way a good work avails through the manner of merit whose root is charity. But in the second way the work of one avails the other through the manner of satisfaction, since one can satisfy for another if the former so intends.[65] And such value is understood to be in prayers which are made in order that through them men may be freed from the debt of punishment. And so we must say that prayers made in this latter manner avail only for those for whom they are made and, if many prayers are made for someone he is more quickly freed from the punishment of Purgatory than others for whom they are not made, even if they brought equal sins with them. But we must concede that prayers made for one avail for all inasmuch as all who know rejoice out of charity in the good things that are done out of charity. And in this sense it is true that the prayers avail more for those for whom they are not made if these have greater charity.

Therefore, to the first it must be said that the punishment of being cut off from the divine vision, either absolutely or for a time, is not as such (*per se*) due for a venial sin since it does not involve a turning away from God, but that some are delayed from the divine vision for a time happens accidentally, because as long as they are deserving of any punishment they cannot participate in the highest happiness which consists of the vision. Justice, howevers, considers a punishment due as such (*per se*) for a sin, not however that which follows accidentally.

Through this the response to the second is clear.

We concede the third and likewise the fourth. However, those who are found alive at the end of the world will have few sins needing

---

[65] Satisfaction, an integral part of penance, is recompense for an injury. It removes a past fault by punishing it and preserves against future fault. Because it presupposes an inequality, it is a concern of divine vindictive justice. See *Supplementum*, q. 12, a.2 and a.3, Leonine ed., vol. 12.

cleansing, having been purged by preceding tribulations. It will also be accomplished so that the painfulness of the punishment for a moderate amount of time makes up for the length of punishment in others.

Parallel passages: Quodlibet 7, q. 5, a.2; *Suppl.*, q. 71, a.12.

* * *

QUESTION 8: Two questions were asked concerning the forgiveness of sins:
1. whether a sin against the Holy Spirit is unforgiveable?
2. whether a crusader who dies before he can take the journey across the sea has full forgiveness of sins?

Article 1: Whether a sin against the Holy Spirit is unforgiveable?

On the first we proceed as follows: it seems that a sin against the Holy Spirit is unforgiveable, for the dignity and majesty of the Father, Son, and Holy Spirit are one. But a sin against the Son is not unforgiveable, for Matthew 12:32 says, "Whoever has spoken a word against the son of man, it will be forgiven him." So a sin against the Holy Spirit is not unforgiveable.

But to the contrary: it is said in the same place, "Whoever has spoken a word against the Holy Spirit, it will not be forgiven him either in this world or in the one to come."

I answer: it must be said that a sin against the Holy Spirit has been spoken of in three ways. For teachers before Augustine understood a sin against the Holy Spirit to be a blasphemy against the Holy Spirit or its works, or even against the divinity of God the Father or the Son, because in the common sense the Holy Spirit is also Father and Son, because God is spirit as John 4:24 says.[66] However, they understand a sin against the Son of Man to be a blasphemy against Christ according to his human nature. And the Jews sinned against Christ in both ways. They sinned against him in the first way by attributing the

---

[66] The teachers before Augustine to whom he refers are Athanasius, Hilary, Ambrose, Jerome, John Chrysostom. See ST 2-2, q. 14, a.1, Blackfriars ed., 32: 118.

miracles which he performed through the Holy Spirit and by the power of his divinity to the prince of demons. They sinned against him in the second way saying, "Behold, a gluttonous man, a drunkard, and a friend of publicans," Matthew 11:19. Therefore, Chrysostom calls this second blasphemy forgiveable since they had an excuse because of the weakness of the flesh that they saw in Christ, but he calls the other blasphemy unforgiveable because they had no excuse since they saw clear signs of the Holy Spirit and divinity.[67] Because of this, according to him, this blasphemy was not forgiven those who persevered in it, either in this world or in the one to come, for in this world they were punished for it through the Romans, and in the one to come they will be tortured in hell.

According to Augustine, forgiveness of sins is attributed to the Holy Spirit which is the charity of the Father and the Son.[68] Therefore, he sins against the Holy Spirit or blasphemes who says the word in his heart, mouth, or work and who does this unrepentant to the end of his life in such a way that forgiveness of sins is not granted him. And then it is plain that this sin against the Holy Spirit is not forgiven either in this world or in the world to come.

Modern teachers indeed said that because power is attributed to the Father, wisdom to the Son, and goodness to the Holy Spirit, a sin from weakness is a sin against the Father, a sin from ignorance is a sin against the Son, a sin from a fixed malice is a sin against the Holy Spirit.[69] Therefore, because ignorance or weakness excuses a sin either wholly or partly, they say that a sin against the Father or the Son is forgiven because it either totally lacks fault or it lessens the fault. Malice indeed does not excuse a sin but makes it worse and therefore a sin against the Holy Spirit is not forgiven either wholly or partly because it does not have in itself any aspect of forgiveness to lessen the fault. And if it is sometimes forgiven this is due more to the

---

[67] John Chrysostom, *Commentarius in sanctum Matthaeum evangelistam*, Hom. 41, and Hom. 42, no. 3, PG 57: 449.

[68] Augustine, *Sermones ad populum (de scripturis)*, 71 (on Matth. 12:32), c. 12, PL 38: 454, no. 19.

[69] For example, Richard of St. Victor, *De spiritu blasphemiae*, PL 196: 1187. For St. Thomas, a sin from fixed malice (*certa malitia*) is a sin from habit or a sin through the removal of some prohibitive factor like fear. See ST 1-2, q. 2 and q. 3, Blackfriars ed., vol. 16.

pity of a forgiving God who cures even incurable diseases than to the remissibility of the sin.

And through this the solution to the objections is clear.

Parallel passages: ST 2-2, q. 14, a.3; 3, q. 86, a.3, ad 2; 2 *Sent.*, d. 43, a.4; *De ver.*, q. 24, a.11, ad 7; *De malo*, q. 3, a.15; *In Matth.*, c. 12; *Ad Rom.*, c. 2, lect. 1.

Article 2: Whether a crusader who dies before he takes the journey across the sea has a plenary indulgence for his sins?

On the second we proceed as follows: it seems that a crusader who dies before he takes the journey has full indulgence for his sins.[70]

1. For in order that an indulgence avail someone, it is required that he be truly penitent and confessed, as the papal letter says. Now a crusader who dies before he has taken the journey has all these things which are required according to the form of the letter for the receiving of full indulgence for his sins. Therefore, he receives it fully.

2. Further, only God forgives sins as far as the fault is concerned, so when the pope gives an indulgence for all sins this is not to be referred to the fault but to the totality of the punishments. Therefore, he who takes the cross according to the form of the papal letter will suffer no punishment for his sins and so he will ascend to heaven at once accompanied by full forgiveness of his sins.

But to the contrary:

3. Augustine says in *De trinitate* 15 that removing the sword is not the same thing as healing the wound.[71] For the sword of sin is removed through forgiveness of sin; however the wound is healed through the refashioning of God's image which is accomplished through works of satisfaction. But the crusader who dies before taking the journey underwent no labor towards the refashioning of

---

[70] Indulgences avail for the remission of punishments left after contrition, absolution, and confession. Some particularly meritorious individuals have performed supererogatory works of penance and suffered many trials unjustly through which punishments could be expiated. But these were not needed for expiation in their cases. Such merits then comprise a treasury which can be drawn upon by the pope when he or someone authorized by him issues indulgences. The total collection of merits exceeds the punishments due the living, see *Supplementum*, q. 25, a.1, Leonine ed., vol. 12.

[71] Augustine, *De trinitate* 14, c. 17, no. 23, CC 50A: 454, lines 6-8; PL 42: 1054-1055.

his image so the wound is not yet healed and he will not be able to arrive in glory at once before suffering the punishments of Purgatory.

4. Moreover, any priest uses such words: "I absolve you from all your sins." Therefore, if the dying crusader should rise to glory, for the same reason so would any other person absolved by any priest. This is incoherent.

I answer: it must be said that, in order to clear up this question, the work of one person can satisfy for another to whom it is referred through the intention of the one performing it, as we said above in article 1. However, Christ shed his blood for his Church and did and suffered much else besides, the estimate of which is of infinite value because of the worth of the person suffering. Hence it is said in Wisdom 7:14 that "there is an infinite amount" in that "treasury for men." Likewise, all the other saints had the intention in the things they suffered and did for God's sake that these would not only be useful for them but also for the whole Church. Therefore, the whole treasury is in the dispensation of him who rules the universal Church, since the Lord committed to Peter the keys of the kingdom of heaven (Matthew 16:19). So when the welfare or necessity of the Church itself demands this, he who rules the Church can share with someone who through charity becomes a member of the Church as much as seemed suitable to him from that infinite treasury, either to the total forgiveness of punishments or up to some determined quantity – and in such a way that the suffering of Christ and the other saints is imputed to this person as though the himself had suffered as much as sufficed for the forgiveness of his sins, just as happens when one satisfies for another, as we said.

Therefore, for indulgence to avail someone three things are needed: first a cause pertaining to God's honor or the Church's necessity or welfare; second the authority in the one who grants indulgences, for the pope can do so principally and others can inasmuch as they receive either ordinary or committed, that is delegated power from him; third that he who wants to receive the indulgence be in a state of charity. And these three conditions are designated in the papal letter. For the appropriate cause is designated in what was premised concerning the aid of the Holy Land, the authority indeed in that mention is made of the authority of the apostles Peter and Paul and of the pope himself, the charity of the recipient in these words, "To all penitents and confessed people." It does not say, "and those making satisfaction" because an indulgence does not excuse one from contrition and confession but takes the place of satisfaction.

Hence we must say to the question proposed that if, according to the form of the papal letter, an indulgence is conceded to those taking the cross in aid of the Holy Land, a crusader has an indulgence at once, even if he dies before he takes the journey. However, if it is contained in the form of the letter that an indulgence be given those who cross the sea, he who dies before he crosses lacks the cause of the indulgence.

Therefore, to the first it must be said that in this last case, that which is more principal, namely the cause of the indulgence, is lacking in the dying crusader.

To the second it must be said that only God forgives a fault through authority, but a priest does also by his ministry insofar as he confers a sacrament of the forgiveness of sins, for example in baptism or in penance. However, an indulgence is not extended for forgiveness of a fault because it is not something sacramental since it does not result from orders but jurisdiction.[72] For a nonpriest can also grant an indulgence if it is committed to him to do so and therefore, the punishment is wholly remitted if the cause is there but not if it is wanting.

To the third it must be said that satisfaction is both punitive inasmuch as it is an act of vindictive justice, and also medicinal inasmuch as it is something sacramental. So an indulgence takes the place of satisfaction as punitive, because the punishment which another suffers is imputed to this person as though he himself had suffered, and therefore the guilty condition of punishment is removed. But it does not take the place of satisfaction as medicinal, because the propensities to commit sins which are left from a prior sin remain, and for the healing of these the labor of satisfaction is more necessary. And therefore, crusaders while they live must be counseled not to neglect works of satisfaction inasmuch as they

---

[72] By ordination someone receives the power of orders, i.e., the power to administer the sacraments. The power of jurisdiction, on the other hand, is obtained by appointment. There are keys of orders and of jurisdiction. The former is something sacramental while the latter are not. Remission through indulgence can be obtained by the keys of jurisdiction for it is a matter of dispensing the common goods of the Church, not the sacraments. See *Supplementum*, q. 25, a.2, ad 1, Leonine ed., vol. 12.

preserve from future sins, although the guilty condition of punishment be totally removed. Nor is any labor required for this because the labor of Christ's suffering suffices. However, such preservation is not necessary for the dying, but only liberation from the guilty condition of punishment.

To the fourth it must be said that the priest's saying "I absolve you from all your sins," is not related to punishment but to fault for the absolution of which he devotes his ministry. However, no one can be absolved from one fault without being absolved from all. Punishment can be dismissed totally or in particular – in particular indeed in sacramental absolution, totally in the spiritual grace of an indulgence, as the Lord says to an adulterous woman in John 8:11: "I will not condemn you. Go and sin no more."

Parallel passages: Quodlibet 5, q. 7, a.2; 4 *Sent.*, d. 20, q.1, a.3; qc 3, ad 2.

Bibliography

I

The following works pertain to quodlibetal disputes in general or to the *Quodlibetal Questions* of St. Thomas in particular.

Axters, E. "Où en est l'état des manuscrits des questions quodlibétiques de saint Thomas d'Aquin?" *Revue thomiste* 19 (1936), 505-530.

——. "Pour l'état des manuscrits des questions quodlibétiques de Thomas d'Aquin." *Divus Thomas* 41 (1958), 293-301.

Beltrán de Heredia, Vicente. "Estudios criticos sobre los cuodlibetos de D. Thomas." *La ciencia tomista* 29 (1924), 371-386.

Boyle, Leonard E. "The Quodlibets of St. Thomas and Pastoral Care." *The Thomist* 38 (1974), 232-256.

Castagnoli, Pietro. "Le dispute quodlibetali vii-xi di S. Tommaso." *Divus Thomas* 31 (1928), 276-296.

Chenu, M.-D. *Toward Understanding St. Thomas*. Tr. A. M. Landry and W. D. Hughes. New York: H. Regnery, 1964, pp. 91-93 and 285-287.

Deman, T. "Éclaircissements sur Quodlibet viii, a. 13." *Divus Thomas* 38 (1935), 42-61.

Denifle, H. "Die Statuten der Juristen-Universität Bologna, I." *Archiv für Literatur und Kirchengeschichte des Mittelalters* 3 (1907), 196-347.

Destrez, J. "Les disputes quodlibétiques de saint Thomas d'après la tradition manuscrite." *Mélanges thomistes*. Kain: Le Saulchoir, 1923. 1: 61-66.

Driscoll, A. M. *The 'Quaestiones Quodlibetales' of St. Thomas Aquinas*. (Dissertation). Washington: Catholic University, 1930.

Glorieux, Palémon. "Aux origines du Quodlibet." *Divus Thomas* 38 (1935), 502-522.

——. "L'enseignement au Moyen Âge. Techniques et méthodes en usage à la Faculté de théologie de Paris au xiiie siècle." *Archives d'histoire doctrinale et littéraire du Moyen Âge* 43 (1968), 65-186.

——. *La littérature quodlibétique de 1260 à 1320*, 1 and 2. Kain: Le Saulchoir, 1925, and Paris: Vrin, 1935.

——. "Où en est la question du Quodlibet?" *Revue du Moyen Âge latin* 2 (1946), 405-414.

——. "Le plus beau Quodlibet de S. Thomas (ix), est-il de lui?" *Mélanges de science religieuse* 3 (1946), 235-268.

——. "Le Quodlibet et ses procédés rédactionnels." *Divus Thomas* 42 (1939), 61-93.

——. "Les Quodlibets vii-xi de S. Thomas d'Aquin. Étude critique." *Recherches de théologie ancienne et médiévale* 13 (1946), 282-303.

——. "Le Quodlibetum XII de saint Thomas." *Revue des sciences philosophiques et théologiques* 16 (1927), 20-46.

Grabmann, Martin. *Die Werke des Hl. Thomas von Aquin.* In *Beiträge zur Geschichte der Philosophie und Theologie des Mittelalters* 22, 1-2: 282-285. Münster: Aschendorff, 1931.

——. "Indagini e scoperte intorno alla cronologia della ... Quodlibeta." *San Tommaso d'Aquino: Publicazzione commemorativo del sesto centenario della canonizzazione.* Milano: Univ. Catt. del S.C. Milano, 1923, 100-121.

Isaac, Jean. "Le Quodlibet 9 est bien de S. Thomas." *Archives d'histoire doctrinale et littéraire du Moyen Âge* 22-23 (1948), 145-185.

——. Review of Pelster's "Literarhistorische..." in *Bulletin thomiste* 8 (1947-1953), 169-172.

Joyce, T. A. "The *Quaestiones quodlibetales* of St. Thomas Aquinas." *Dominicana* 16 (1931), 13-18.

Mandonnet, P. "Chronologie sommaire de la vie et des écrits de saint Thomas." *Revue des sciences philosophiques et théologiques* 9 (1920), 142-152.

——. *Des écrits authentiques de saint Thomas d'Aquin.* Fribourg: S. Paul, 1910.

——. Preface, *S. Thomas Aquinatis Quaestiones quodlibetales.* Paris: Lethielleux, 1925, v-viii.

——. *Siger de Brabant et l'Averroïsme latin au 13e siècle.* 2 vols. 2nd ed. Louvain: 1908 and 1911, vols. 6 and 7 in *Les philosophes belges,* 1: 85-87.

——. "Thomas d'Aquin, créateur de la dispute quodlibétique." *Revue des sciences philosophiques et théologiques* 16 (1927), 5-38 and 15 (1926), 477-506.

Meier, L. "Les disputes quodlibétiques en dehors des universités." *Revue d'histoire ecclésiastique* 53 (1958), 401-442.

Motte, A. R. "La chronologie relative du Quodlibet VII et du commentaire sur le IVe livre des Sentences." *Bulletin thomiste* 7 (1931-1933), 29-45.

Pelster, F. "Beiträge zur Chronologie der Quodlibeta des Hl. Thomas von Aquin." *Gregorianum* 8 (1927), 508-538; 10 (1929), 52-71, 387-403.

——. "Literarhistorische Probleme der Quodlibeta des Hl. Thomas von Aquin, I and II." *Gregorianum* 28 (1947), 78-100; 29 (1948), 62-87.

——. "Wann ist das zwölfte Quodlibet des Hl. Thomas von Aquin entstanden?" *Gregorianum* 5 (1924), 278-286.

Steenberghen, F. van. *Siger de Brabant dans l'histoire de l'aristotélisme.* Louvain, 1942, p. 541.

Synave, P. "L'ordre des Quodlibets VII à XI de S. Thomas d'Aquin." *Revue thomiste,* n.s. 9 (1926), 43-47.

——. Review of Destrez. *Bulletin thomiste* 1 (1924), 32-50.

——. Review of Pelster's "Beiträge zur Chronologie der Quodlibeta des Hl. Thomas von Aquin" in *Bulletin thomiste* 2 (1930), 48.

Walz, Angelus. *Saint Thomas Aquinas: A Biographical Study.* Tr. S. Bullough. Westminster, Md.: The Newman Press, 1951, 73-75.

Weisheipl, James A. *Friar Thomas d'Aquino: His Life, Thought, and Work*. New York: Doubleday & Co., Inc., 1974, pp. 105-106, 126-128, 212, 363, 367-368.

II

The authors or works below are cited by St. Thomas. Occasionally he does not cite them by name but simply as 'some' or '*quidam*'.

Albert the Great. *Scripta super iv libros sententiarum*. In *Opera omnia*. Ed. A. Borgnet. Paris: Vives, 1890-1899, vols. 25-29.

Ambrose. *Expositio evangelii secundum Lucam*. Ed. M. Adriaen. cc 14. Turnholti: Brepols, 1957; pl 15: 1607-1944.

Anselm. *De casu diaboli*. In *Opera omnia*. Ed. F. S. Schmitt. Edinburgh: T. Nelson, 1946-1961, vol. 1.

Aristotle. *The Works of Aristotle*. Ed. W. D. Ross. London: Oxford University Press, 1908-1952. 12 vols.

Augustine. *De civitate dei*. Ed. B. Dombart and A. Kalb. cc 47-48. Turnholti: Brepols, 1955; csel 40; pl 41.

——. *De doctrina christiana*. Ed. J. Martin. cc 32. Turnholti: Brepols, 1962; pl 34: 15-122.

——. *De Genesi ad litteram*. Ed. Jos. Zycha. csel 28: 3-435. Vienna: Tempsky, 1894; pl 34: 245-486.

——. *De gestis Pelagii*. Ed. Urba and Zycha. csel 42: 51-122. Vienna: Tempsky, 1913; pl 44: 319-360.

——. *De gratia Christi*. Ed. Urba and Zycha. csel 42: 125-206. Vienna: Tempsky, 1913; pl 44: 359-386.

——. *De libero arbitrio*. Ed. Wm. Treen. csel 74. Vienna: Tempsky, 1956.

——. *De trinitate libri xv*. Ed. W. J. Moutain. cc 50-50a. Turnholti: Brepols, 1968; pl 42: 819-1098.

——. *Enchiridion ad Laurentium*. Ed. M. van den Hout, et al. cc 46. Turnholti: Brepols, 1969; pl 40: 231-290.

——. *In Iohannis evangelium tractatus cxxiv*. Ed. R. Willems. cc 36. Turnholti: Brepols, 1954; pl 35: 1379-1976.

——. *Sermones ad populum*. pl 38, 39.

——. *Sermones de vetere testamento. Id est, Sermones [ad populum] i-l*. Ed. C. Lambot. cc 41. Turnholti: Brepols, 1961.

Averroes. *Aristotelis opera cum Averrois commentariis*. Venice: Juntas, 1562-1574; repr. Frankfurt: Minerva, 1962. 11 vols.

Avicenna. *Avicennae opera*. Venice, 1508; repr. Frankfurt: Minerva, 1962.

——. *Avicenna latinus: Liber de anima*. Ed. S. Van Riet. Leiden: Brill, 1968.

Basil. *Contra Eunomium*. pg 29: 497-774.

Bernard of Clairvaux. *Sancti Bernardi opera*. Ed. J. Leclercq and H. Rochais. Rome: Editiones Cistercienses, 1957 – ; pl 182-185.

Biblia sacra cum glossis, interlineari et ordinaria cum expositione Lyre. No place, 1588. 6 vols.

Boethius. *The Theological Tractates*. Ed. E. K. Rand. Cambridge, Mass.: Loeb Classical Library, 1918; repr. 1962; PL 64: 1247-1354.

Cicero. *De officiis*. Ed. and trans. W. Miller. Cambridge, Mass.: Loeb Classical Library, 1913.

Eadmer. *Liber sancti Anselmi De similitudinibus*. PL 159: 605-708.

Glossa ordinaria. PL 113-114. Also see *Biblia sacra*... above.

Gratian. *Decretum. In corpus iuris canonici*. Ed. A. L. Richter. Lipsiae: B. Tauchnitz, 1839. Vols. 1 and 2; PL 187.

Gregory the Great. *Dialogorum libri IV*. Ed. U. Morrica. Rome: Tip. del Senato, 1924; PL 77: 147-432.

———. *Moralia in Iob*. Ed. M. Adriaen. CC 143-143A. Turnholti: Brepols, 1979; PL 75: 509 - 76: 782.

———. *Quadraginta homiliarum in evangelia libri duo*. PL 176: 1077-1314.

Hilary of Poitiers. *De trinitate*. Ed. P. Smulders. CC 62. Turnholti: Brepols, 1980; PL 10: 25-472.

Isidore of Sevile. *Synonyma*. PL 83: 827-868.

Jerome. *Commentariorum in Matheum libri IV*. Ed. D. Hurst and M. Adriaen. CC 77. Turnholti: Brepols, 1969; PL 26: 15-218.

John Chrysostom. *Commentarius in sanctum Matthaeum evangelistam*. PG 57.

Peter Lombard. *Collectanea in omnes D. Pauli Apostoli epistolas*. PL 191: 1297 - 192: 520.

———. *Libri IV sententiarum*. 2nd ed. Quaracchi: Typographia Collegii S. Bonaventurae, 1916. 2 vols.; PL 192: 519-962.

Prepositinus. *Summa*. In *Opera omnia*. *Revue des sciences philosophiques et théologiques*. Kain (Belgium): Le Saulchoir, 1927 - .

Richard of St. Victor. *De spiritu blasphemiae*. PL 196: 1185-1194.

William of Auxerre. *Summa aurea in quattuor libros sententiarum*. Paris, 1500; repr. Frankfurt: Minerva, 1964.

III

Other Works Cited

Complete editions of St. Thomas's Works:

St. Thomas Aquinas. *Opera omnia*. Leonine ed. Rome: Typographia Polyglotta, 1882-19 - .

———. *Opera omnia*. Parma: Fiaccadori, 1852-1873; repr. New York: Musurgia, 1948-1950. 25 vols.

———. *Opera omnia*. Paris: Vives, 1871-1872. 34 vols.

Anthologies:

An Aquinas Reader. Ed. Mary T. Clark. New York: Doubleday, 1972.

The Pocket Aquinas. Ed. Vernon J. Bourke. New York: Washington Square Press, 1965.

St. Thomas Aquinas Theological Texts. Ed. Thomas Gilby. New York: Oxford University Press, 1955.

Individual works by St. Thomas:

Compendium theologiae. Leonine ed., vol. 42. Rome: Typographia Polyglotta, 1976.

Contra errores Graecorum. Leonine ed., vol. 40. Rome: Typographia Polyglotta, 1967.

De ente et essentia. Ed. C. Boyer. Rome: Universitas Gregorianae, 1970. Also Leonine ed., vol. 43. Rome: Typographia Polyglotta, 1976.

De perfectione spiritualis vitae. Leonine ed., vol. 41. Rome: Typographia Polyglotta, 1970.

De principiis naturae. Leonine ed., vol. 43. Rome: Typographia Polyglotta, 1976.

De spiritualibus creaturis. Ed. L. Keeler. Rome: Universitas Gregorianae, 1946.

De substantiis separatis. Ed. F. J. Lescoe. West Hartford, Conn.: St. Joseph College, 1962.

De virtutibus in communi; De caritate; De correctione fraterna; De spe; De virtutibus cardinalibus. Ed. E. Odetto. Taurino: Marietti, 1953.

Expositio et lectura super epistolas Pauli apostoli. Taurino: Marietti, 1953. 2 vols. (*Ad Hebr.; Ad Rom.; Ad Tit.; I Tim.; I ad Cor.*).

Expositio in librum Boethii de hebdomadibus. Taurino: Marietti, 1954.

Expositio super Dionysium de divinis nominibus. Ed. C. Pera and P. Caramello. Taurino: Marietti, 1950.

In Aristotelis librum de anima commentarium. Ed. A. M. Pirotta. Taurino: Marietti, 1948.

In xii libros metaphysicorum expositio. Ed. M.-R. Cathala. Taurino: Marietti, 1935.

Postilla super Psalmos. Parma ed., vol. 14; Vives ed., vol. 18.

Quaestiones de anima. Ed. J. H. Robb. Toronto: Pontifical Institute of Mediaeval Studies, 1968.

Quaestiones disputatae de malo. Ed. R. Bazzi and P. M. Pession. Taurino: Marietti, 1953.

Quaestiones disputatae de potentia. Ed. P. M. Pession. Taurino: Marietti, 1953.

Quaestiones disputatae de veritate. Leonine ed., vol. 22. Rome: Typographia Polyglotta, 1970-1974.

Quaestiones quodlibetales. Ed. R. Spiazzi. Taurino: Marietti, 1956. Also Parma ed., vol. 9, and Vives ed., vol. 15.

Scriptum super libros sententiarum. Ed. P. Mandonnet and M. F. Moos. Paris, 1929-1947. 4 vols.

Summa contra gentiles. Leonine ed., vols. 13-15. Rome: Typographia Polyglotta, 1918-1930.

Summa theologiae. Latin text and English translation. New York: Blackfriars in conjunction with McGraw-Hill, 1964-1969. 60 vols.

Super evangelium Matthaei expositio. Ed. P. Raphael Cai. Taurino: Marietti, 1951.

Super evangelium Johannis lectura. Ed. P. Raphael Cai. Taurino: Marietti, 1952.

120 BIBLIOGRAPHY

Supplementum to Summa theologiae. Leonine ed., vol. 12. Rome: Typographia Polyglotta, 1906.

Works by other authors:

Augustine. *De haeresibus.* Ed. M. van den Hout, et al. CC 46. Turnholti: Brepols, 1969.

Avicebron (Solomon Ibn Gabirol). *Fons vitae.* Ed. C. Baeumker. *Beiträge zur Geschichte der Philosophie des Mittelalters,* Band 1, Hefte 2-4. Münster: Aschendorffschen, 1891-1895.

Bettoni, Efrem. *St. Bonaventure.* Tr. A. Gambatese. Notre Dame: University of Notre Dame Press, 1964.

Bobik, Joseph. *Aquinas on Being and Essence: A Translation and Interpretation.* Notre Dame: University of Notre Dame Press, 1970.

St. Bonaventure. *Commentaria in iv libros sententiarum.* In *Opera theologica selecta,* vol. 1. Quaracchi: apud Collegium S. Bonaventurae, 1934.

Bourke, Vernon J. *Aquinas' Search for Wisdom.* Milwaukee: The Bruce Publishing Co., 1965.

Callus, Daniel. "The Origins of the Problem of the Unity of Form." *The Thomist* 24 (1961), 257-285.

Copleston, Frederick. *A History of Philosophy.* New York: Doubleday, 1962, vol. 2.

Edwards, Sandra. *Medieval Theories of Distinction.* Unpublished dissertation. Philadelphia: University of Pennsylvania, 1974.

———. "St. Bonaventure on Distinctions." *Franciscan Studies* 38 (1978), 194-212.

Gilson, Étienne. *Being and Some Philosophers.* 2nd ed., corr. and enlarged. Toronto: Pontifical Institute of Mediaeval Studies, 1952.

———. *The Christian Philosophy of St. Thomas Aquinas.* Tr. L. K. Shook. New York: Random House, 1966.

———. *History of Christian Philosophy in the Middle Ages.* London: Sheed and Ward, 1955.

———. *La théologie mystique de St. Bernard.* Paris: J. Vrin, 1934.

Grajewski, Martin. *The Formal Distinction of Duns Scotus.* Washington, D.C.: The Catholic University Press, 1944.

John Duns Scotus. *Opera omnia.* Ed. L. Wadding. Hildesheim: Olms repr., 1968.

Kendzierski, Lottie H. Introduction to her translation of St. Thomas's *On Charity.* Milwaukee: Marquette University Press, 1960, pp. 1-6.

Klubertanz, George P. *St. Thomas Aquinas on Analogy.* Chicago: Loyola University Press, 1960.

Lamb, Matthew. Notes to his translation of St. Thomas's *Commentary on St. Paul's Epistle to the Ephesians,* pp. 306-309. Albany, N.Y.: Magi Books, 1966.

McInerny, Ralph. *The Logic of Analogy.* The Hague: M. Nijhoff, 1961.

Mascall, Eric L. *Existence and Analogy.* London: Longmans, 1949.

Maurer, Armand. Introduction to his translation of St. Thomas's *On Being and Essence*. Toronto: Pontifical Institute of Mediaeval Studies, 1968, pp. 7-27.

Murphy, John L. *The General Councils of the Church*. Milwaukee: The Bruce Publishing Co., 1959.

New Catholic Encyclopedia. Editorial Staff of Catholic University of America. New York: McGraw Hill, 1967. 17 vols.

Owens, Joseph. "Analogy as a Thomistic Approach to Being." *Mediaeval Studies* 24 (1962), 303-322.

——. "Common Nature: A Point of Comparison between Thomistic and Scotistic Metaphysics." *Inquiries into Medieval Philosophy*, ed. J. F. Ross, pp. 185-209. Westport, Conn.: Greenwood Pub. Co., 1971.

——. "Quiddity and Real Distinction in St. Thomas Aquinas." *Mediaeval Studies* 27 (1965), 1-22.

——. "Thomistic Common Nature and Platonic Idea." *Mediaeval Studies* 21 (1959), 211-223.

Oxford Dictionary of Christianity. Ed. by F. L. Cross. London: Oxford University Press, 1974.

Phelan, Gerald B. *St. Thomas and Analogy*. Milwaukee: Marquette University Press, 1941.

Pieper, Josef. *Guide to Thomas Aquinas*. Tr. by R. and C. Winston. New York: The New American Library, 1964.

Ross, James F. "A New Theory of Analogy." *Proceedings of the American Catholic Philosophical Association* 44 (1970), 70-85.

Sharp, D. E. *Franciscan Philosophy at Oxford in the Thirteenth Century*. London: Oxford University Press, 1930.

Index of Sources Cited by St. Thomas

General Index

Maurer, A. 21 n58
mendicants 10-11
merit 44, 45, 48
ministers 102-103
miracles 71-72; and Christ 87-90
mixture 43
monks 66-68
motion 37, 38-39, 49 and time 85-87

nature 80-82; and individual or supposit: see essence; human 17, 74; of sin 63-64
Nestorius 33 n12

obedience 60-63, 66-68, 98-99
offices, Church 55-57
Owens, J. 21 nn56 & 58, 23 n63, 80 n13

papal constitutions 65-66
papal letter 111, 113
parents 90-94, 98-99
Paris, University of 1ff.
participation 79
Pelagians 44-45
Pelster, F. 5, 11 n17, 6
penance 49-55; see also confession, contrition, satisfaction
perfection, state of 11-12, 59-60
perjury 64-65
person 73-74, 76
Phelan, G. 80 n13
place 36-39, 68-72
power, of orders and of jurisdiction 113
Praepositinus 107 n64
prayers 106-109
preachers 102-103
precepts 53, 64-65, 67-68; judicial, moral, ceremonial 95-97
predication 18-19, 22-23; accidental 13, 82-83; analogous, equivocal, univocal 79-80 n13; essential and through participation 18-19, 78-79; per se and per accidens 13-14, 22, 82-83

prelates 57, 59, 61-63, 67-68, 101-102
price, just 75, 76
priests 11-12, 54, 55, 59-60
principles, essential 83, 84
privation 63-64
punishment 49, 50, 62, 64-65, 66, 68, 104-106
purgatory 106-109

quodlibetal disputes 3-5

redemption 76
relation 30-34
religious 11-12, 59-63, 66-68
Richard of St. Victor 110 n69
Ross, J. F. 80 n13

sacraments 51-52
sameness, numerical 16-18, 42, 73, 74; real 21; specific 42
satisfaction 108, 111-114
secrets 60-61
Sharp, D. 15 n36, 16 n42
Silvester, Pope 92
sin 44, 49-54, 55, 62, 63-64, 65-66, 101-102, 109-111; forgiveness of 109-111
soul 16, 17, 35-36, 40-43, 80, 82; Christ's 73-74; powers of 14, 40-43, 104-106
species 79, 83-84
Spiazzi, R. 3 n11, 24-25
state (status) of perfection 11-12, 59
Steenberghen, F. van 5, 6
substance 19, 79, 81, 84
substantial form: see form
supposit 17, 81-82; and see individual

teaching 57-60
Theodosius 92
theology, teachers of 57-60; study of, and teaching of, at University of Paris 1ff.
Thomas Aquinas, St., academic career at University of Paris 1-5;